Art of Island Southeast Asia

Art of Island Southeast Asia

The Fred and Rita Richman Collection

in

The Metropolitan Museum of Art

Florina H. Capistrano-Baker

With an Introduction by Paul Michael Taylor

The Metropolitan Museum of Art

Published in conjunction with the exhibition *Divine Protection: Batak Art of North Sumatra*, The Metropolitan Museum of Art, New York, April 22–December 31, 1994

Copyright © 1994
The Metropolitan Museum of Art, New York

Published by
The Metropolitan Museum of Art, New York

John P. O'Neill, Editor in Chief
Barbara Burn, Executive Editor
Emily Walter, Editor
Elizabeth Finger, Designer
Peter Antony, Production Manager

Photography by Carmel Wilson,
The Photograph Studio,
The Metropolitan Museum of Art

Map drawn by Irmgard Lochner.

Illustrations appearing on pages 29, 63, and 73 are courtesy the Vereinigte Evangelische Mission, Wuppertal-Barmen.

Set in Sabon, with Gill Sans Bold display by Southern New England Typographic Service, Hamden, Connecticut
Printed on 80lb Lustro Dull
Printed by Mercantile Printing Company, Worcester, Massachusetts
Bound by Acme Bookbinding Company, Charlestown, Massachusetts

Library of Congress Cataloging-in-Publication Data
Capistrano-Baker, Florina H.
    Art of island Southeast Asia : the Fred and Rita Richman Collection / Florina H. Capistrano-Baker ; with an introduction by Paul Michael Taylor.
        p.   cm.
    Includes bibliographical references.
    ISBN 0–87099–697–5.
    ISBN 0–87099–698–3 (pbk.).
    ISBN 0–8109–6484–8 (Abrams)
    1. Decorative arts—Indonesia—Catalogs.   2. Decorative arts—Asia—Catalogs.   3. Folklore in art—Indonesia—Catalogs.   4. Folklore in art—Asia—Catalogs.   5. Richman, Fred—Art collections—Catalogs.
6. Richman, Rita—Art collections—Catalogs.   7. Decorative arts—Private collections—New York (N.Y.)—Catalogs.   8. Decorative arts—New York (N.Y.)—Catalogs.   9. Metropolitan Museum of Art (New York, N.Y.)—Catalogs.   I. Title.
NK1059.C36   1994
730'.09598'0747471—dc20   93–51050
                                                    CIP

Frontispiece

Pupuk container, North Sumatra (Batak), 19th–20th century. Ceramic, wood. H. 13 1/2 in. (34.4 cm). Gift of Fred and Rita Richman, 1988 (No. 20)

Jacket/cover illustration

Si gale-gale, North Sumatra (Batak), 19th–20th century. Wood, metal. H. 11 1/4 in. (28.6 cm). Gift of Fred and Rita Richman, 1987 (No. 27). Photograph by Bruce White

Contents

Foreword   6
Philippe de Montebello

Collectors' Note   8
Fred and Rita Richman

Acknowledgments   10

Map: Island Southeast Asia   12

Introduction: Island Southeast Asia   13
Paul Michael Taylor

Catalogue   21
Florina H. Capistrano-Baker

Checklist of the Collection   116

Glossary   148

References Cited   150

Foreword

The Metropolitan Museum of Art is once again indebted to the generosity of private donors for initiating commitment to a field of collecting that is new to the Museum. In 1988, Fred and Rita Richman gave to the Metropolitan a collection of Island Southeast Asian art that was the first of its kind to enter the Museum. Produced by the indigenous peoples of the many islands that make up this western Pacific region, the works in the Richman Collection were brought together over a period of twenty years. The visual power and formal simplicity of the art of the island peoples were compelling to the Richmans, and they sought to learn about its makers at the same time as they collected the works themselves. Because the Richmans had benefited from their dual interests in distant peoples and their extraordinary artwork, they wished to share both with a larger public.

The attentive reader of these pages will find that Island Southeast Asia is made up of more than 17,000 islands, including the modern nations of the Philippines, Indonesia, Brunei, and eastern Malaysia. Art from some areas of the mainland is included in this collection, because it is cultural and stylistic affinities and not geography that are the defining features. A common language, and a culture in common, may at an early time have unified the peoples of this vast region, and in spite of incursions, invasions, displacements, colonialism, and contact with no fewer than four of the world's great religions (Hinduism, Buddhism, Islam, and Christianity), a commonality remains. The visual arts illustrate this tenacious unity.

Many different island peoples are represented by works in this catalogue. Among those of most significant presence are the Batak peoples who live in the northern part of the Indonesian island of Sumatra. The Batak had a pervasive belief system that imbued their traditional art with profound meaning. Many of their works were rendered powerful by natural and supernatural forces; funerary monuments, guardian figures, architectural elements, ritual paraphernalia — all invoked sacred protection, enhancing the earthly power and prestige of their owners and users.

Together with the thanks the Museum owes to the Richmans for their generous gift of 1988, thanks must also go to Douglas Newton, Curator of Oceanic Art and Evelyn A. J. Hall and John A. Friede Chairman of the department at the time of the gift, for his long devotion to the art of the Pacific islands. It is a field of growing presence at The Metropolitan Museum of Art.

PHILIPPE DE MONTEBELLO
Director
The Metropolitan Museum of Art

Collectors' Note

In the winter of 1952 I made my first visit to Indonesia, primarily to test the market for textiles of American manufacture. At that time, Indonesia was emerging from years of colonization by the Dutch and subsequent conquest by the Japanese during World War II, and the Indonesians were just getting their first taste of *merdeka* (freedom) in the twentieth century. I had only a limited knowledge of art in general then and knew nothing of the art of Indonesia in particular. Little did I realize that twenty years later my wife, Rita, and I would begin to put together a collection of the art of the indigenous peoples of that part of the world.

Initially, our journey into the field of collecting followed the general route of Western civilization, beginning, as we did, with biblical and Near Eastern antiquities and going on to the classical world of Greece, Etruria, and Rome. One of the gems of that early collection was a Cycladic idol dating to about 2000 B.C. Our love for that simple, stylized sculpture would soon lead us into other areas, away from the naturalistic art of Greece and Rome.

On a trip I made to Turkey in 1967, I had the good fortune to meet a very knowledgeable American collector of African art, another field that was foreign to us. We bought our first piece of African art that year, as a novelty, a diversion from classical sculpture. As we explored further, we began to sense a similarity in feeling between some African art and the Cycladic idol, and we realized that our taste ran to sculpture that was elemental both in form and in style.

We shifted our collecting emphasis to Africa. For the next eight or ten years, we traveled, read, studied, learned about, and collected African art, uncovering worlds new to us, the history of peoples and kingdoms, their movements and migrations, their trade and religions.

While traveling in Europe in the spring of 1976, we bought in Paris a small, beautifully carved bottle stopper just four inches high in the form of a horse and rider. We were not certain where it had come from, but we thought it was of Tschokwe origin, from Angola in Central Africa. We showed it to a number of dealers in Europe and were eventually informed that it was carved by the Batak people of Sumatra, Indonesia.

Who were the Batak people? What other ethnic groups inhabited Indonesia? What did their art look like? These and a thousand other questions came to be answered as we embarked on a new quest, one that started in Holland. The museums in Amsterdam, Leiden, and Delft provided the beginnings of our knowledge. Art dealers in Holland, Belgium, and France provided more. We then made an extended trip to Indonesia, which put everything in context.

As we collected, we continued to read and to study. We were fascinated by such writers as Robert Heine-Geldern, who described trade patterns and migrations of peoples. Our explorations allowed us to follow through the centuries cultural and artistic patterns from such diverse regions as the steppes of the Ural Mountains in Russia and the jungles of Indochina. Of particular interest was the commonality of art styles that extended all the way from Madagascar, off the east coast of Africa, to the Philippines and Taiwan.

Early in 1988 I discussed with Douglas Newton, then the Evelyn A. J. Hall and John A. Friede Chairman of the Department of Primitive Art at the Metropolitan Museum, the fact that the Museum, despite the depth and breadth of its collections, did not own any indigenous Indonesian art. It became clear to me that our collection should go to the Museum to fill that void. There, it would serve the community far better than if it were to remain displayed in our home on Long Island. The gift was officially made later that year, and an exhibition of selected works opened in June 1989, continuing until September of that year.

For my wife and me, the forty years that have passed since my first trip to Indonesia have been years inspired by a broadening of knowledge and a deepening of our appreciation of the art and culture of many varied peoples. It is our hope that the collection, housed at the Metropolitan, will do the same for all those who will now have the opportunity to visit it there.

FRED AND RITA RICHMAN

Acknowledgments

This catalogue and the art collection that it documents owe their existence to the foresight and generosity of Fred and Rita Richman. The book was first conceived during the tenure of Douglas Newton as Evelyn A. J. Hall and John A. Friede Chairman of what is now the Department of the Arts of Africa, Oceania, and the Americas. Julie Jones, Curator in Charge, made it a reality. I thank them all for their trust.

The book is the result of a collaborative effort among many individuals. Emily Walter, Senior Editor, embraced the project with characteristic dedication. Her perceptive comments and suggestions regarding content and style played a vital role in the shaping of the text. Carmel Wilson, Photographer, devoted her expertise to capturing the sculptural qualities of the objects. The elegant presentation of the material is the work of Elizabeth Finger, Designer. Peter Antony, Production Manager, expertly shepherded the book from the initial stages of photography to its successful completion. Jean Wagner carefully edited the bibliographical citations; and Mary W. Smith, Computer Specialist, provided valuable technical assistance. The project was supervised by Barbara Burn, Executive Editor. I wish also to thank my colleagues in the Department of the Arts of Africa, Oceania, and the Americas, who provided not only friendship and moral support but were always forthcoming with insightful comments and advice.

I am grateful to colleagues and museum staff in Southeast Asia, Europe, and the United States, who generously opened their storerooms and shared museum records. In Indonesia, Dra. Kartiwa Suwati, Director of the National Museum, Jakarta, provided access to the resources and staff of the regional museums in Sumatra. Drs. Erman Makmur and Ita Malik of the Museum Adityawarman, West Sumatra, Dra. Wardjana Anwar and Anurlis Abbas of the Universitas Andalas, and Syahriwal and Endri provided transportation, hospitality, friendship, and guidance.

In Germany, Heide Koch and Barbara Faulenbach of the Vereinigte Evangelische Mission, Wuppertal-Barmen, facilitated study of early missionary collections, documents, and photographs. Dr. Johanna Agthe of the Museum für Völkerkunde, Frankfurt am Main, allowed me to study and photograph the Batak and Nias objects. Dr. Rose Schubert of the Museum für

Völkerkunde, Munich, granted generous access to the Indonesian collection and warm friendship in a foreign land. At the Koninklijk Instituut voor de Tropen (Royal Tropical Institute), the Netherlands, I thank J. H. van Brakel of the Tropenmuseum, and Henk van Rinsum of the Photo Archiv.

In the United States, I wish to thank Dr. David Hicks, of the State University of New York at Stony Brook, and visiting scholar Dr. Elena Soboleva, of the Russian Academy of Sciences, for brief but informative discussions pertaining to the art of Timor. I am grateful to Dr. Bennet Bronson, Curator of Asian Ethnology at the Field Museum of Natural History, Chicago, for giving me access to the Batak objects and for generously giving of his time and insights. I take this opportunity to thank also a friend and an inspiration, Dr. Harold Conklin of the Department of Anthropology, Yale University, whose pioneering interest and scholarship in Island Southeast Asia helped lay the foundations for projects such as this one.

Finally, I wish to express heartfelt thanks to family members without whose constant support this book could not have been completed. In particular, my deepest gratitude to Thomas and Natividad Parris and their children, John, Cristina Laura, and Patricia, and to Isabel Dimayuga. I thank my husband, Kendal, and our daughter, Phoebe, for their patience and love, and for their companionship during several research trips abroad.

FLORINA H. CAPISTRANO-BAKER

Island Southeast Asia

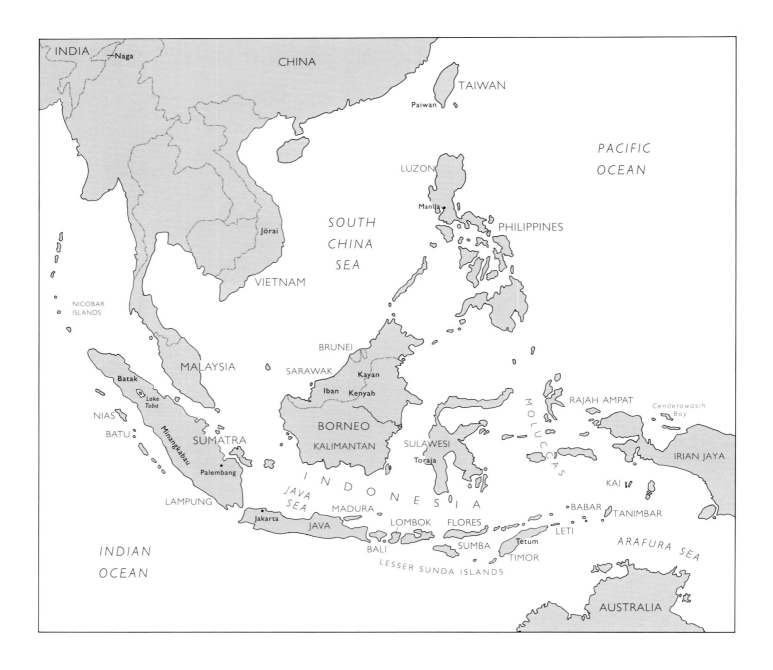

Introduction: Island Southeast Asia

PAUL MICHAEL TAYLOR

The art of Island Southeast Asia is relatively little known in the West. This book, based on works in the collection of Fred and Rita Richman, is one of a number of scholarly contributions to this growing area of study. We begin on the central Indonesian island of Borneo and move on to the region's island groups in ever-wider concentric arcs. Traveling first westward to Sumatra and Nias and then eastward past Sulawesi to Irian Jaya's north coast, the Moluccas, and Lesser Sunda Islands, we proceed to the mainland to examine the indigenous art of Assam and of central Vietnam, and, traveling southeast, we return to the islands, to Taiwan and the Philippines.

To provide a broad context for the collection, this essay briefly introduces the geography and cultural history of the region and the concept of Island Southeast Asia as a cultural entity.[1] Also known as insular Southeast Asia, the region inconveniently crisscrosses many contemporary political boundaries. Its heartland lies in Indonesia, and indeed the Richman Collection is particularly rich in objects from Borneo and Sumatra. The same mountain chain that forms Sumatra's backbone dips under the sea as it crosses the unmarked border between Indonesia and India, then emerges farther north as the Nicobar and Andaman archipelagoes. Regional affinities also extend north of Indonesia throughout Southeast Asia's other great archipelagic nation, the Philippines, to the aboriginal peoples of Taiwan, and even to such mainland peoples as the Jörai of Vietnam and the peoples of the Naga hills in Assam, India.

Island Southeast Asia is the term increasingly used for the region that, in the earlier literature, was referred to as the Malay Archipelago, Indonesia, or Malaysia, in the broadest sense of those terms. The term Malay Archipelago was inadequate because Malays are only one of the region's hundreds of ethnic groups, and because Indonesia and Malaysia have now been adopted as names for nations. Island Southeast Asia has thus been increasingly accepted as a term for this culture area, even though it includes related mainland peoples as well. The region comprises one of the five standard parts of Oceania (the Pacific islands), the other four being Melanesia, Polynesia, Micronesia, and Australia. The dual aspect of its identity is aptly expressed in its name, sprawled as it is within Oceania's island realm and yet historically in continuous contact with events and influences from the Asian mainland. The region minimally includes the modern nations of the Philippines, Indonesia (except Irian Jaya), Brunei, and the eastern part of Malaysia (Sarawak and Sabah). Within Oceania, Island Southeast Asia is generally distinctive for precisely those products that arise from its association with the Southeast Asian mainland, such as weaving, metallurgy, and grain-crop staples. And religious systems from the mainland, namely Hinduism, Buddhism, and Islam, initially provided an ideological basis for the region's bureaucratically organized kingdoms and other forms of sociopolitical organization.

Attempts at compartmentalizing the region's cultural diversity, like attempts at partitioning its history into distinct periods, are fraught with difficulties, and naturally many areas overlap. The richness of the region's heritage depends on its deep Austronesian, or Oceanic, roots mixed with influences from the Indianized and other Asia-influenced civilizations of the mainland. The influence of Asian cultures on the Austronesian peoples can, to some extent, be traced in its movement eastward. Yet many parts of Island Southeast Asia never developed the bureaucratically organized kingdoms or urban centers that we associate with Asia. And many regions on the mainland remained isolated, or were repopulated by people who had abandoned urban regions and then regrouped in tribal forms of political organization. Such groups include the tribal peoples of Vietnam and the Naga of Assam, whose artistic production, as exemplified here, is sometimes identified stylistically with Island Southeast Asia.

Even the earliest attempts to identify cultural similarities within this region included areas of mainland Asia. When Grégoire Louis Domeny de Rienzi first introduced the elements of the five-part division of Oceania (which he considered the "fifth part" of the world, after Europe, Africa, America, and Asia), in a lecture to the Geographical Society of Paris in 1831,[2] he proposed a culture area which reflected the fact that ethnic groups in Taiwan, Madagascar, and present-day western Malaysia all spoke Austronesian languages, and the name Malaysia (or Malaisia, as it was also known) soon came to denote the entire region.

Active trade with China, India, mainland Southeast Asia, and the Middle East has characterized the region for over two thousand years. Since the 1500s, starting with the Spanish, Portuguese, and Dutch, contact with the West has also been important, and the twentieth century has witnessed the decline of colonialism and the rise of new nations, which have postcolonial characteristics of their own.

Because the majority of objects in the Richman Collection are from present-day Indonesia, we shall consider that country in greater detail.

Indonesia: Geographical and Historical Influences

Indonesia's islands are commonly divided into four major groups. The Greater Sunda complex, lying atop the suboceanic Sunda shelf, includes the major islands of Sumatra, Java, Borneo, Sulawesi, and such smaller islands as Bali and Madura. The Lesser Sundas complex is formed by the island chain that continues through oceans east of Bali, from Lombok to Timor. The Moluccas (or Maluku) form the third region, which is composed of deep seas interspersed with volcanic islands and uplifted blocks at the border of the Euro-Asian and Indo-Australian continental plates. The fourth area is Irian Jaya, on the western (Indonesian) half of the continental island of New Guinea, which sits atop the Sahul shelf and is linked to Australia across the Arafura Sea.

Indonesia straddles the equator between the Philippines to the north and Australia to the south, from the Indian Ocean in the west eastward to New Guinea, and covers some 1,100 miles from north to south and 3,200 miles from west to east. Its land area of 741,000 square miles makes Indonesia the world's eighth largest nation. With over 188,000,000 people, it is the world's fourth largest country by population. Cartographers of the Dutch colonial era counted the well-known figure of 13,677 islands; since the introduction of satellite images, however, smaller specks of land have been observed and figures of more than 17,000 islands have been suggested.

The tropical rain forests, the predominant natural vegetation over most of Indonesia and nearly all of Island Southeast Asia, are associated with warm temperatures year round and heavy rains without a marked dry season. Over the past two centuries, however, population growth and logging have virtually wiped out primary forests on Java, much of Sumatra, and Bali, and the rain forests are being cut down at an alarming rate on many other islands as well. Peoples of nearly all Indonesian ethnic groups practice agriculture, although a preagricultural form of subsistence economy is practiced by a few hunter-gatherer groups that sparsely populate the forested interiors of some of the outer islands.

Among the many generalizations that have been offered about the effects of ecology and habitat on Island Southeast Asia's cultural traditions, one of the most important is associated with two alternative forms of agriculture practiced by peoples throughout the region: swidden, or slash-and-burn, as opposed to wet-rice agriculture. Wet-rice agriculture, which is capable of sustaining much higher population densities, predominates on Indonesia's inner islands of Bali, Java, and nearby Madura; swidden agriculture predominates on the outer islands, whose peoples created most of the works represented in this catalogue. It should be added that this distinction also admits exceptions. Wet-rice agriculture has spread rapidly in outer-island regions over the past century, and some outer-island regions had wet-rice cultivation in antiquity.

Within Indonesia, the difference in agricultural methods partly explains the huge population disparity between the inner and the outer islands, and has been put forward to explain some differences in traditional forms of social organization. The inner islands (Java and the two tiny islands of Bali and Madura) are home to 58 percent of Indonesia's population, though they make up only 7 percent of the nation's land area. Population density seems inversely related to cultural diversity; only a handful of languages are spoken on the inner islands, whereas nearly all of Indonesia's over three hundred languages are spoken on the outer islands. Clifford Geertz has pointed out that wet-rice

Terraced wet-rice fields, Bali, 1988.
Photograph by Amir Sidharta

agriculture has the potential for large increases in yields as labor inputs increase, so that an increasingly dense population can live off the same amount of land by putting greater and greater amounts of labor into a small plot.[3]

In wet-rice agriculture, nutrients are brought in by means of highly regulated irrigation systems. Clearing a forest to make a wet-rice field is like creating a miniature ecological aquarium in which labor-intensive tending and careful feeding are rewarded by increased productivity. In societies based on this agriculture, such as the court societies of central Java, dense populations and a high level of regional coordination developed to guarantee appropriate irrigation.

In swidden agriculture, by contrast, the plot's vegetation is cut and burned and nutrients are added in an ashy layer that is quickly depleted after a few years of crop cultivation, which can require that the plot then lie fallow for several decades. Because of the limitations on population growth imposed by this form of agriculture, outer-island societies never developed dense populations and the forms of political organization that evolved could more often be characterized as bands, tribes, or chiefdoms. The different types of social organization associated with these two agricultural systems have long been recognized on mainland Southeast Asia as well.[4]

The archipelago comprises thousands of islands, some of which fall within volcanic arcs and have mountainous areas separated by valleys and lowlands, providing sheltering refugia, or regions protected by their isolation, for vast numbers of plant and animal species. It has been argued that Indonesia's impressive cultural diversity (measured by the more than three hundred languages spoken in the region[5]) is due in part to the physical isolation of its island regions and in part to parallel variations in fauna and flora, which offer niches for human populations. Such interpretations are appealing, though they are difficult to prove.

Swidden field of rice and other
crops, Halmahera, Moluccas, 1978.
Photograph by Paul Michael Taylor

Indonesia's seas have, paradoxically, both maintained the isolation of its peoples and united them. A long history of inter-island communication has tended to make the life-styles of coastal populations similar to one another through an exchange of ideas and products that has helped them adapt to the coastal environment. The highland peoples on the island interiors have remained more isolated from one another, though their contact with down-river, coastal peoples, who themselves communicate with other parts of the archipelago, has provided broader contacts for them as well. Yet the sea has also prevented mass migrations, and together with the interior terrain, which is difficult to traverse, it has undoubtedly enabled small ethnic groups to survive as distinct entities and, over the millennia, to develop a rich linguistic and cultural diversity.

In the same way that these geographical facts have promoted cultural diversity, they have diminished centralized political control. In a few remote outer-island areas, tribal groups are still virtually independent. Such autonomy most likely predominated throughout the region prior to the development, under the influence of Buddhism and Hinduism, of larger kingdoms during the period of Indianized states. From the seventh to the fourteenth century, the Buddhist kingdom of Srivijaya flourished on Sumatra. At its peak, the Indianized Srivijaya empire reached as far as West Java and the Malay Peninsula. By the fourteenth century, however, the Hindu kingdom of Majapahit had risen in eastern Java and gained control over most of what is now modern Indonesia.

Historians prior to the 1960s cited civilizing and empire-building migrations, or waves of influence, from India and mainland Southeast Asia to explain this period of Indianization, though documented evidence of migration and conquest is lacking. More recently, there has been speculation that leaders within Indonesian chiefdoms imported foreign religions such as Buddhism and Hinduism to bolster their claims to divine kingship.[6] Islam, which had a foothold in Indonesia by the twelfth century, had widely replaced Hinduism on Java and Sumatra by the end of the sixteenth century. On Bali and a few other islands even today, however, Hinduism is still practiced. At the present time, approximately 88 percent of the Indonesian population is Muslim, 9 percent is Christian, and 2 percent is Hindu.

Prehistory

Many historians have attempted to establish a prehistoric substratum of Indonesian art by a subtractive method, that is, by first identifying the Asian, Middle Eastern, and European elements within Indonesian art, and then "subtracting" them and imagining what art forms and traditions might have been like prior to those influences. A more effective method of obtaining data on the earliest forms of Indonesian art, however, is through archaeological investigation. The earliest objects excavated in the region are pottery from the Lapita Pacific island cultures (1500–500 B.C.) and bronze ware from the Vietnamese culture of Dongson (600 B.C.–A.D. 100). These finds indicate that there were indeed travel and trade throughout the archipelago as early as the second millennium B.C. Notable similarities exist between geometric designs seen in Indonesia and designs from these early cultures. The early Austronesian-speaking peoples who migrated from the Southeast Asian mainland eastward through the Pacific islands and into Indonesia, Melanesia, and Polynesia may have been Lapita cultures, though they may, on the other hand, have developed independently in the Pacific, possibly near the Bismarck archipelago.[7]

The Dongson culture flourished from about 600 B.C. to A.D. 100 in the Tonkin region of Vietnam, and bronze artifacts from this culture have been found throughout Indonesia, from Sumatra to Irian Jaya. New theories of an independent Indonesian origin for certain design motifs or of a common Southeast Asian artistic heritage are also being formulated. That a common artistic heritage existed is strongly supported by both the Lapita pottery and the Dongson bronzes; design motifs may, however, have been transmitted on such trade items as textiles, which disintegrated over time, leaving no trace.

Linguistic evidence also supports a common prehistoric Austronesian protoculture. Bellwood has hypothesized that early non-Austronesian-speaking peoples whose languages included prototypes of some of the present-day Papuan and Austro-Asiatic languages were displaced by a prehistoric expansion of Austronesian-speaking peoples through Southeast Asia, the Philippines, and eventually Indonesia.[8] The origin of the Austronesian groups that moved throughout the Pacific Bellwood believes to have been a group of Proto-Austronesian-speaking migrants from mainland South China that migrated to Taiwan and developed a language he terms Initial Austronesian. He further suggests that Proto-Austronesians settled on Taiwan by about 4000 B.C., after which their Initial-Austronesian-speaking descendants moved into the Philippines. By 2500 B.C., Proto-Austronesians were heading south into the Indonesian archipelago. The spread of Austronesians was so extensive throughout the archipelago that today nearly all ethnic groups of the region speak Austronesian languages.

The only non-Austronesian languages spoken in Indonesia today are the so-called Papuan languages of Irian Jaya, Halmahera and Morotai, Timor, Alor, and Pantar — all presumably spoken by the descendants of ethnic groups not supplanted by Austronesian-speaking peoples during the waves of Austronesian migrations.[9] The term Papuan has been applied to all non-Austronesian languages of this region on the grounds that they may originally have been related, though similarities between them today are insufficient to consider them all descendants of a single protolanguage.

Autochthones and the Search for Origins

Indigenous art and material culture have always been recognized as sources of information about the people who produced them. Increasingly, collections of such art are also being analyzed as expressions of the cultures of the collectors. Such collections are developing an informed and critical audience, not only in cosmopolitan urban centers but also in the rural and island regions in which they originated.

The art of small-scale societies is sometimes referred to as tribal, archaic, or primitive. The use of such terms, however, no matter how qualified with favorable adjectives, perpetuates a postcolonial view of this art as evolutionally antecedent to, rather than simply different from, Western art forms.[10] The traditional artists of Island Southeast Asia and those for whom traditional arts are expressions of their own local identity do not of course recognize any of these categories.

Traditional art is associated by collectors in Western cultures with several assumptions. Minimally, they include the following: that traditional art is an expression of people closer than we are to the original state of humankind, and thus appeals at an elemental level; that it is produced by autochthones, people native to a region and thus closely connected to the land (the term "autochthone" derives from the Greek *auto*, meaning "self," and *chthon*, meaning "ground"; thus, "sprung from the ground"); that it represents traditions which are extinct or in imminent danger of extinction; and that it is thus increasingly difficult to obtain and is in its nature different from contemporary art.

Each of these assumptions contains both accuracies and inaccuracies. But more important is their increasing effect on both the production of art in its region of origin and the appreciation of that art. The search for the "original state" of these art forms is also reflected in the so-called subtractive method, described above.

The link between indigenous societies and political scale also influences the distinction made in Western society between what we refer to as tribal art and what we refer to as folk art. Tribal art represents traditions from isolated, semi-independent cultures, like those thought to have evolved first in human prehistory. Folk art represents traditions from the rural component of societies that are both urban (or courtly) and rural and which are mutually dependent on one another. Indonesian art historians today use the term "traditional arts" (*seni tradisional*) to refer to both folk and tribal traditions.

Indonesians are baffled at the second assumption, that the creators of this art, in being native to the region, are somehow more closely connected to the land. Javanese, for example, would emphatically and justifiably reject the notion that they are less native to their locale than tribal peoples. Throughout Indonesia, traditional art is becoming increasingly popular, since for the descendants of the peoples who produced it, the art represents renewed expressions of their ethnic identity within the modern Indonesian state.

The third assumption is that these art traditions are extinct or disappearing. But, in fact, though some forms have not survived, many have merely been transformed. Most of the objects in this collection date from the late nineteenth and early twentieth century, a period of extensive contact with Europeans, as a result of which widespread changes occurred. In general, traditional art of this period is now being treated by Southeast Asians as a classical period in its own right, one that provides a rich visual vocabulary that today's artists are increasingly using to reinforce their own regional identity in a modern context.

1. A more detailed summary of Indonesian geography and history may be found in my essay "Indonesia: Jewel in the Crown" (Taylor 1994b). This essay's discussion of prehistory follows the treatment Lorraine V. Aragon and I presented in *Beyond the Java Sea* (Taylor and Aragon 1991). For a close examination of the topics discussed in the section "Autochthones and the Search for Origins," readers are referred to Taylor 1994a.

2. Domeny de Rienzi 1836, pp. 11–14.

3. See Geertz 1963.

4. On this subject, see, for example, Burling 1965.

5. Counting the number of languages in a given region is a generally accepted method of estimating the number of ethnic groups. The Indonesian Language Development Proj-ect has estimated that approximately 350 languages are spoken in Indonesia. By contrast, Grimes (1988) lists 669 living and three known extinct languages. Such divergent estimates are the result of different approaches to the determination of language-dialect boundaries, whether, for example, the speech forms of two communities are defined as two different languages or two different dialects of the same language.

6. Soedjatmoko, Resink, and Kahin 1965.

7. For a discussion of these processes, see Bellwood 1985 and Kirch and Hunt 1988.

8. Bellwood 1985, pp. 102–29.

9. Wurm and Hattori 1983, pp. 28–34.

10. See Taylor and Aragon 1991, pp. 18–19. By contrast, Hersey (1991) prefers the term "primitive."

Catalogue

Introduction to the Catalogue

FLORINA H. CAPISTRANO-BAKER

Images . . . have, apart from their manifest motifs, often a hidden meaning, not immediately realized. . . . They owe their complexity to the very fact that their meaning is not perfectly or not immediately clear.[1]

The Fred and Rita Richman Collection is both a valuable historical record and an impressive assemblage of art made in Island Southeast Asia during the late nineteenth and early twentieth century. Many of the art forms represented here no longer survive, and those that do are seldom created in their original context, for the local peoples have mostly converted to religious beliefs different from those that originally dictated their creation. Similarly, the social context in which these art forms were traditionally made has been altered by new economic and political institutions introduced during the colonial period, from the sixteenth to the early twentieth century.

The art in this collection represents a dynamic period in history when the European demand for spices, silks, and other exotic luxuries irreversibly altered the lives of the peoples of Island Southeast Asia. Western intervention commenced early in the sixteenth century, when the Portuguese successfully found an eastward route around Africa to the fabled Spice Islands of the East Indies—the Moluccas in present-day Indonesia—and established a permanent trading post there. The Spaniards followed in 1521, when Ferdinand Magellan "discovered" and claimed for the Spanish crown the archipelago that was to become the modern nation of the Philippines, named after King Philip II of Spain. In the late sixteenth century, the Dutch wrested control of most of the Indonesian islands—which they called the Dutch East Indies—from their Portuguese rivals, successfully establishing a lucrative world monopoly of the spice trade. The French, who had broken the Dutch trade monopoly in the eighteenth century, colonized Vietnam on the mainland, while the British controlled present-day Malaysia, Singapore, and India.

As a result of Europe's mercantile exploits in the region and the inevitable social, political, and economic changes introduced by Western colonization, the majority of the local populations now call themselves and their homelands by names determined by their former colonizers, subscribe to foreign religious beliefs, and generally renounce the old ways as backward. Traditional beliefs in the supernatural and the art objects that had figured so prominently in ritual contexts are no longer completely understood. And contemporary interpretations by local peoples are often informed by an overlay of Islamic or Christian doctrine.

The art of Island Southeast Asia is not a static entity but continuously changing and evolving. One important indicator of such change is the discrepany between interpretations and terminology documented in late-nineteenth and early-twentieth-century accounts and contemporary field data.[2] The arts of the different islands are formally and conceptually related, deriving from shared ethnic, linguistic, and cultural sources. These affinities cut across present-day political boundaries, a lasting legacy of the region's colonial past, when competing European powers imposed artificial borders that remained even after the colonies had attained independence. Borneo, for example, the third largest island in the world, is today divided politically among three different nations. Formerly a British protectorate, the ancient kingdom of Brunei on the north coast, which lent the island its name, is now an independent country; the Federation of Malaysia has political jurisdiction over Sabah and Sarawak, the former British colonies of North Borneo and Northwest Borneo, the home of the Kenyah and Kayan peoples; and the Republic of Indonesia governs the larger section of the island, Kalimantan, formerly a part of the Dutch East Indies and home of other Kenyah and Kayan groups related to those across the Malaysian border. Because this book is concerned with affinities and continuities, the independent nations that now have jurisdiction over the various cultural groups that produced the work have been temporarily set aside.

One highly visible manifestation of the close ties among the peoples of Island Southeast Asia are convergences in their art. The meanings assigned to similar art forms and their stylistic renderings vary throughout the region, but the basic concepts are universal. Four major motifs illustrate these commonalities. Broadly stated, the art addresses two fundamental concerns, fertility and protection. Four important visual images that evoke these themes are the seated human figure (nos. 1, 3–10, 17, 29, 37, 45–48), the omega-shaped ornament called *mamuli* in East Sumba (nos. 51, 52), the water buffalo (no. 34), and the *naga*, or serpent-dragon (nos. 19, 43), which also takes the form of a composite creature called *singa* in North Sumatra (nos. 14, 15, 32).

A major sculptural tradition in Island Southeast Asia, the seated or squatting human figure usually portrays an ancestor, a spirit, or a deity. Animated by the supernatural, such figures played an active role in the world of the living, accepting ritual offerings, dispensing advice, and bestowing protection. The significance of the figures' flexed posture has been the subject of much speculation among Western scholars. One interpretation points to an analogy with the fetal position. Another explanation refers to the flexed burial position used for high-ranking individuals. In the scholarly quest to decipher complex symbolic associations, the obvious is sometimes overlooked. Local peoples familiar with the old ways will easily recognize the replication of a common posture assumed by the living while engaged in a host of activities such as chewing betel nut, partaking of meals, or participating in community meetings and ceremonies. The spirits, actively involved in the daily affairs of human beings, naturally assumed a similar posture.

Of the earliest art forms known in Island Southeast Asia, the distinctive omega-shaped ear ornament known as *mamuli* in East Sumba, and by other names elsewhere, is among the most intriguing. Jade versions dating from about 1000 B.C. to A.D. 1 have been found at archaeological sites in Taiwan, Vietnam, and the Philippines.[3] More recent examples in gold, silver, and brass are found throughout the region, such as the *lingling-o* of Northern Luzon and the *taiganja* of Sulawesi. The ornament's omega shape, evoking female reproductive organs, expresses the fundamental interest in human fecundity, which embraces the more universal theme of growth and, by extension, agriculture. Such jewelry was at the same time invested with protective powers, expressed in the generic word for earrings, *anting-anting*, which also means "protective charm." Certain types of *mamuli* were, in fact, imbued with such significance that they were used by diviners and priests as mediators between the spirit and the human worlds.[4]

Concern with agricultural growth and abundance is also expressed in the image of the water buffalo, an important beast of burden that was not only indispensable in the cultivation of rice but was also a prestigious sacrificial offering. Water buffalo horn trophies displayed on house gables commemorated the great numbers of animals slaughtered and distributed among the members of the community at ritual feasts, thus signifying the owner's wealth. Most frequently seen in architectural ornamentation, the buffalo horn motif also translates into smaller objects, such as headdresses (no. 34) and jewelry. The horn itself was used for symbolically potent objects, such as ritual containers (nos. 19, 32) and sword handles (no. 31).

Practically synonymous with Island Southeast Asian art, the *naga* plays an important role in different myths throughout the region. Derived from the Sanskrit word for snake, the *naga* is often identified with the sea serpent and the underworld in the mythology of many mainland and Island Southeast Asian cultures. Other reptiles, such as lizards (no. 25) and crocodiles, being amphibious creatures associated with both land and water, possessed supernatural powers and frequently served as symbols of fertility and regeneration. In many Southeast Asian cultures, such creatures also function as protective beings. On Borneo, the *naga* manifests itself as the serpentine *aso*, or dog, motif (no. 12), an apotropaic device to ward off evil. On Sumatra, *naga* is transformed into *singa*, a mythical being that combines aspects of the water buffalo, horse, and serpent-dragon. Like the *naga*, the *singa* is associated with supernatural power and protection.

Complex associations and overlapping meanings of related motifs are no longer fully understood. One doubts that they were ever completely known, except perhaps by the ritual specialist. Interpretations have become even more blurred with the passage of time, manifested in the changing meanings of local words. The Batak term *pangulubalang*, for example, was consistently documented in the late nineteenth century to denote the powerful captive spirit of a ritually executed human being. Contemporary Batak and Western scholars now use the word to refer to anthropomorphic sculpture imbued with the powers of the *pangulubalang*, objects previously referred to by the generic term *gana-gana* (no. 26). Without losing sight of these limitations to our understanding of forms and their meanings, one is, nevertheless, able to discern certain fundamental human concerns that guide the creation of such works. Interpretations and formal aspects of the motifs discussed above and represented in this catalogue may differ in details, but always they return to notions of earthly fertility and protection through supernatural intervention. Art in precolonial Southeast Asia was, after all, born of the need to conjoin spirit worlds and island realms.

1. Hauser 1985, p. 101.

2. The complex issues of changing forms and meanings are explored in greater depth in Capistrano-Baker, n.d.

3. Solheim 1981, p. 44.

4. Rodgers 1985, p. 63.

The indigenous peoples of the island of Borneo, collectively known as the Dayak, built large, communal longhouses along the banks of major rivers and tributaries.[1] *Hampatong*, or protective figures, guarded the entrances to their villages and houses. This imposing *hampatong* depicts a male figure seated on a tall, necked jar. According to Dayak belief, figurative representations dispelled evil spirits and brought good fortune. Each *hampatong* was carved for a specific purpose and personified a particular spirit or deity. This figure's elaborate headdress and the replication in wood of the prestigious *martaban* jar suggest that it probably represents a deceased person of high rank.[2] The spirit of the deceased had to inhabit the *hampatong* before it could begin its long and dangerous journey to the next world. In addition to anthropomorphic figures, images of protective creatures such as tigers, bears, and leopards were also carved for funerals of important persons.[3]

The figure's tranquil naturalism distinguishes it from other types of *hampatong*, which are characterized by such exaggerated features as bulging eyes or an aggressively protruding tongue (no. 2). The large imported *martaban* jar on which the figure sits was usually displayed prominently in the family room. *Martaban* were used for storing rice and wine, and as burial containers. A storage vessel that had been reserved for funerary use was placed upside down to indicate that the owner did not wish to have it used for other purposes.[4] Such jars were also placed on top of funerary posts in mausoleum complexes.

1. The generic name Dayak includes different indigenous groups such as the Kenyah, the Kayan, and the Iban.

2. The term *martaban*, which refers to large ceramic jars manufactured in China as well as to imitations made in various Southeast Asian kilns, derives from the lower Burmese port of Martaban, where such vessels were either traded or manufactured. Maritime trade between Burma (present-day Myanmar) and the Indonesian islands extends back to the early eleventh century. By the mid-fourteenth century, the large ceramic storage jars had already acquired the generic name *martaban*, regardless of their place of manufacture. The fourteenth-century Arab scholar Ibn Batuta recorded the use of such containers in 1350 (Brown 1988, pp. 99–104). Ascribed supernatural powers, the jars were thought to be either male or female and were divided into twelve types according to their decoration. The three most prized were the *gusi*, the *naga*, and the *rusa* (Hein 1890, pp. 133–39). The Dayak themselves do not call these containers *martaban* but use the local names *tempayan*, *djawet*, *blanga*, or *tadjau*, depending on the region (ibid.; Nieuwenhuis 1907, pl. 40).

3. Hein 1890, pp. 30–33.

4. Chin 1988, pp. 61–62.

2

Hampatong

Borneo, Kalimantan (Dayak)
19th–20th century
Wood
H. 44½ in. (113 cm)
Gift of Fred and Rita Richman, 1988
1988.143.1

Exhibited: New York, The Metropolitan
Museum of Art, 1989

Published: Hersey 1980, p. 81; Hersey
1991, p. 18, fig. 9

Hampatong that portray protective beings often have a prominently protruding tongue, such as the one seen here. These figurated posts were frequently put at the house entrance or in the family room to ward off evil spirits and illnesses. They were also placed along paths leading to the houses, or at village boundaries. Special occasions, such as a successful headhunting expedition, the purchase of a prestigious *martaban* jar, or an important person's funeral, called for the manufacture and display of such posts.[1] Influences from mainland Asian cultures are apparent in the use of the lotus upon which the figure sits and in the graceful vegetal motifs carved in relief at the base of the pedestal.

1. Hein 1890, pp. 18, 30–31.

View of a Dayak village. Print, from the reports of the Rheinische Missionsgesellschaft (October 1874)

3

Tuntun

Borneo, Sarawak (Iban)
19th–20th century
Wood
H. 21 in. (53.3 cm)
Gift of Fred and Rita Richman, 1988
1988.143.17

Published: Richman 1980, fig. 1;
Hersey 1991, fig. 34

4–10

Tuntun

Borneo, Sarawak (Iban)
19th–20th century
Wood
Gift of Fred and Rita Richman, 1988

Published: Richman 1980, fig. 1;
Hersey 1991, fig. 34

4

H. 21¼ in. (54 cm)
1988.143.11

5

H. 20 in. (50.8 cm)
1988.143.12

6

H. 21 in. (53.3 cm)
1988.143.13

7

H. 20½ in. (52.1 cm)
1988.143.14

8

H. 22¾ in. (57.8 cm)
1988.143.15

9

H. 21 in. (53.3 cm)
1988.143.16

10

H. 21½ in. (54.6 cm)
1988.143.18

The Iban people used carved measuring rods, or *tuntun*, to determine the correct placement of the deadly pig trap, or *peti*. Because of frequent accidents that resulted in the impalement of humans on the trap's bamboo spear, use of the dangerous hunting device was prohibited by the Sarawak government in the late nineteenth century.[1]

According to Iban mythology, a spirit named Se Genun taught man the art of making *tuntun*, the proportions of which were measured by placing a piece of wood in the crook of the elbow and taking the length to the tip of the middle finger. Spirits that assisted in hunting are represented on the wooden rods. Images similar to nos. 6 and 8, for example, are said to portray Se Genun himself.[2] Another benevolent spirit is Raja Laut, usually depicted seated on a stool and wearing a haji's hat, such as in nos. 5 and 10.[3]

The beauty of the carved image was believed to increase the efficacy of the *tuntun* in luring animals to the trap. Most figures have an open mouth or bared teeth, which represents the spirit's calling out to the pig. Magic bundles of cloth held between the flexed legs of the figures (as in nos. 3, 5, 6, 7, and 9) also helped to ensure success in hunting. The cloth was invested with special powers during a purification ritual in which offerings and invocations were made to the spirits portrayed on the *tuntun*.[4]

1. Roth 1896, p. 439. See also Hose and McDougall 1912, pp. 145–46; Amsterdam, Tropenmuseum, 1987, p. 269, no. 95; Revel-Macdonald 1988, p. 77; and Heppell and Limbang 1988, pp. 64–65. According to the last source, the top of the rod marks the correct height for snaring wild pig, while the top of the carved figure indicates the proper height for the sambhir deer; other notches show the height that should be used for smaller animals, such as the mouse deer. In contrast to Roth (1896, p. 439), who describes such rods as charms that were planted near the pig traps, Heppell and Limbang (1988, pp. 64–65) contend that *tuntun* were not left at the hunting site but brought back to the longhouse, whence they called out to their prey.

2. Heppell and Limbang 1988, pp. 65, 67, figs. 1, 3.

3. A haji is a follower of Islam who has made the pilgrimage to Mecca; he marks the journey by wearing a distinctive costume that features a flat-topped, cone-shaped hat derived from the fez.

4. Heppell and Limbang 1988, p. 66.

11

Hudoq[1]

Borneo, Kalimantan (Kenyah or Kayan)
19th–20th century
Wood, pigment, rattan
H. 17 in. (43.2 cm)
Gift of Fred and Rita Richman, 1988
1988.143.77

Exhibited: New York, The Metropolitan Museum of Art, 1989

Published: Hersey 1980, cover; Hersey 1991, fig. 33

Rice is the most important staple food in Southeast Asia. Among the various Dayak peoples of the Upper Mahakam River area, dance festivals were held shortly after sowing to ensure the proper growth of young rice plants. Young men wearing painted masks would perform the *hudoq* dance, impersonating spirits who had come down to earth to bless and protect the harvest. According to one recent account, the masked dancers would emerge from the forest and converge at the center of the village. Offering seeds believed to contain the soul of the rice to each household, the masked beings brought bountiful rice harvests and bestowed fertility on women. The masks were carefully stored after the agricultural rites, to be painted and decorated anew during the next planting season.[2] The most prestigious type of *hudoq* is the composite dragon-hornbill mask, such as the one seen here.[3] Already exaggerated features are further heightened by painted curvilinear designs, which together with the round, staring eyes, pointed nose, and fanged mouth create an impressive, intimidating presence. The separately carved winglike ears recall similarly constructed serpent masks from Sri Lanka.

1. *Hudoq* means "mask" in Kayan. Variations of the term are *hudo'* in Busang, *udöq* in Kenyah, and *hedoq* in Modang (Revel-Macdonald 1988, p. 85). Among the Busang, all masks are carved from a wood called *plaie*, which is closely linked with fertility because of the association of sap with a mother's milk (Heppell and Maxwell 1990, p. 65).

2. Revel-Macdonald 1978; Revel-Macdonald 1988, pp. 79, 242; Amsterdam, Tropenmuseum, 1987, p. 269, no. 93.

3. Sellato 1989, p. 211, fig. 336. The hornbill, the dragon, and the *naga* (serpent-dragon) all represent important beings in the mythology of many Southeast Asian cultures.

12

Hawat

Borneo (Kenyah or Kayan)
20th century
Beads, rattan, wood, fabric, shell, teeth
H. 13 in. (33 cm)
Gift of Fred and Rita Richman, 1988
1988.143.52

Published: Richman 1980, fig. 4

The autochthonous peoples of Borneo believed that an infant's soul was not yet securely attached to his body.[1] To encourage the spirit to bond more firmly with the infant, the mother performed a ritual each morning and evening in which she would tie the baby's finger to a string attached to the *hawat*, or carrier, and murmur an incantation to lure the soul back to the child.[2] The *hawat* was believed to shelter the infant's spirit, for it was here that the greater part of the early months before walking were spent. A prolonged absence of the soul from the baby's body was believed to cause sickness and even death.[3]

This *hawat* has a wooden base and woven rattan back support. The support is lined with fabric and the outer surface adorned with a bilaterally symmetrical beadwork panel that depicts mirror images of an intertwined avian and canine head, an unusual variation on the *aso*, or dog, motif widely used in Borneo.[4] Additional shell disks, animal teeth, and stringed beads punctuate the sides. The beauty of the *hawat*'s ornamentation was thought to attract benevolent spirits and bring good fortune to the child, while the clinking of the hanging attachments warded off evil. In addition, the design of the beadwork and the materials used to embellish the carrier indicated the social position of the child's family. Only infants born to families of the highest rank, for example, were entitled to use a full-figure motif and hanging attachments of tiger's teeth, the latter being a precious imported item. Children of lesser rank could use only animal-head motifs, such as this one, or abstract curvilinear designs. Contemporary scholarship indicates that such prescriptions survive among the Kenyah today.[5]

1. Nieuwenhuis 1904, p. 71.

2. The *hawat* (Nieuwenhuis 1904, pp. 71–74; Nieuwenhuis 1907, pp. 238–39, 272, pl. 69; spelling variations include *havat* and *avaat*) is also known as *bening* or *benning* in Malayan dialect (Ave 1988; Revel-Macdonald 1978, p. 43), and *ba'* in Kenyah (Whittier and Whittier 1988).

3. Nieuwenhuis 1904, pp. 71–72.

4. This beadwork panel has variously been called *tap hawat* (Nieuwenhuis 1907, p. 272), *inoq aban* (Revel-Macdonald 1978, p. 43), and *aban* (Whittier and Whittier 1988, p. 52).

5. Whittier and Whittier 1988.

13

Hawat

Borneo (Kenyah or Kayan)
19th–20th century
Wood, shell, rattan
H. 12¼ in. (31.1 cm)
Gift of Fred and Rita Richman, 1987
1987.453.2

Published: Delft, Volkenkundig
Museum Nusantara, 1973, fig. 37;
Richman 1980, fig. 5

This *hawat* is constructed entirely of wood. The curved back support features three anthropomorphic figures, each with a heart-shaped face in high relief and a low-relief body in displayed position with outstretched arms.[1] Inlaid shell disks accentuate the eyes and torso. Contemporary fieldwork in Kalimantan indicates that this wooden-type *hawat* is no longer as commonly used today as the beaded rattan version.[2]

The *hawat* played a crucial role in ensuring the well-being of an infant, who was to remain in the house during the first month of life. During this period, the baby received a bracelet made from *bua djele*, a brown-black fruit believed to be effective in warding off evil spirits. When the infant's umbilical cord fell off, this first bracelet was replaced by a second, and then again by a third. The child's mother wore the discarded bracelets around her neck through the first and second name-giving ceremonies, after which they were deposited in a small cotton pouch attached to the *hawat*. At the end of the taboo period, the infant's initial excursion outdoors was taken in the *hawat*, which the mother wore in front during the early months. As the baby grew, she transferred the *hawat* to her back, with the child sitting up against the vertical support, legs wrapped around her waist.[3]

1. A widely used motif in Island Southeast Asia and the Pacific, the displayed position shows the human figure in a squatting posture viewed from the front.

2. Whittier and Whittier 1988, p. 54.

3. Nieuwenhuis 1907, p. 71; Whittier and Whittier 1988, p. 51.

14, 15

Pair of Singa

North Sumatra (Batak)[1]
19th–20th century
Wood
H., each 55 in. (139.7 cm)
Gift of Fred and Rita Richman, 1988
14. 1988.143.27
15. 1988.143.28

Exhibited: New York, The Metropolitan
Museum of Art, 1989

The ornate houses of high-ranking families, substantially larger than those of commoners, flanked the main streets of nineteenth-century Batak villages in North Sumatra. Saddle-shaped roofs whose gabled peaks were surmounted by double-horned water buffalo trophy heads protected the prestigious structures, bringing to mind the architecture of the neighboring Minangkabau people to the south (see no. 34).[2]

These commanding *singa* adorned each side of the facade of a Batak house. Elevated on wooden piles measuring more than six feet high, the upper structure of the house was supported by broad beams called *pandingdingan* that were exposed along the sides of the building. Separately carved *singa* heads were tenoned to the ends of the beams, which served as the reptilian body. Together, the beams and the *singa* were identified with Naga Padoha, the mythical snake of the underworld.[3]

Although the term *singa* derives from the Sanskrit word for lion, the creature called *singa* combines aspects of the water buffalo, horse, and *naga*. *Singa* are sometimes given the form of a buffalo whose body is covered with scales, further reinforcing its affinity with the snake.[4] Such visual devices effectively convey the enigmatic character of these mythical creatures and their metaphorical associations with fertility, abundance, and protection.

1. Much of the Western literature divides the Batak into six ethnic groups: Toba, Karo, Dairi-Pakpak, Simalungun, Angkola, and Mandailing. Rodgers (1985, p. 94) notes that this division is somewhat misleading because the Batak identify themselves in much more local terms as members of a ceremonial league or as inhabitants of village clusters. She further observes that the Batak peoples share many items of material culture; one group, for example, may depend on another group for the manufacture of its ritual objects. Although attempts have been made to attribute a Toba, Karo, or Pakpak provenance to Batak objects such as those in the Richman Collection, such distinctions have been avoided in this catalogue as they are reliable only when documented at the time the object was collected in the field.

2. Giglioli 1893, p. 114; Brenner 1894, p. 264.

3. Amsterdam, Tropenmuseum, 1987, p. 267, nos. 51, 52.

4. By the late nineteenth century, the Batak themselves could no longer explain the origin of the term (Barbier 1983, p. 206, nos. 27, 28).

16

Tunggal panaluan

North Sumatra (Batak)
19th–20th century
Wood, fiber, hair
H. 71 in. (180.3 cm)
Gift of Fred and Rita Richman, 1988
1988.124.1

Exhibited: Dallas, Dallas Museum of
Art, 1982, pl. 28; New York, The
Metropolitan Museum of Art, 1988b,
pl. 10; New York, The Metropolitan
Museum of Art, 1989

Published: Hersey 1980, p. 77

This staff is a classic example of a *tunggal panaluan*, a powerful ritual instrument through which the Batak *datu*, or ritual specialist, protected the village, ensured victory in battle, and called forth rain.[1] A male figure wearing a turban of red, white, and black fiber wrapped around a spray of coarse black hair stands at the top holding a vessel above the head of a second figure, which appears to be a female holding a small animal. Both figures stand on a horselike creature, which in turn stands on another similar creature. A third human figure balances in acrobatic pose between two serpents. A fourth figure is shown, also in acrobatic pose, with another equine creature. A fifth human figure squats underneath. And a sixth figure stands, holding its genitals, near the bottom followed by a buffalo and a series of ridges that may represent reptiles. Most of the figures have small cavities somewhere on their bodies for ritual nourishment.[2]

On the earliest examples known, the uppermost image was always a full human figure with an unusually large head adorned with horsehair and bound with fabric, while the bottom figure was often a serpent wriggling upward.[3] The top figure's head usually had a cavity in which magical substances were deposited.[4] Believed to have originated in the Toba area, the *tunggal panaluan* was used throughout the Batak region.

The figures carved on the staff are generally thought to represent characters in the legend of the incestuous twins Si Adji Donda Hatahutan and his sister, Si Tapi Radja Na Uasan.[5] The many different versions of the myth differ in details, but all follow the same general story, which involves the relationship between the brother and the sister.[6] When the sister is sent away in an effort to break the liaison, her brother searches for and eventually finds her, and together they escape through the forest. There they come upon an enchanted tree, called *pio-pio-tangguhan*. When the brother climbs up the tree to gather fruit for his lover, he is transformed into a wooden image that merges with the tree. Si Tapi Radja Na Uasan follows her brother up the *pio-pio-tangguhan* and suffers the same fate. A succession of *datus* and animals, including a hen, a water buffalo, and a snake, make various attempts to rescue the twins, and they too merge with the tree. Finally, the *pio-pio-tangguhan* is chopped down and images of those trapped are carved into a wooden staff made from its trunk. Because the figures portrayed had all encountered sudden death, their spirits were believed to be extremely potent and were thus invoked to protect the village and to ensure agricultural abundance.

The symbolism of the *tunggal panaluan* has been given many interpretations. It has been suggested, for example, that the relationship between the brother and sister is a metaphor for lightning (male) and rain (female), or lightning-thunder (male) and parched earth (female),[7] while another theory contends that the staff re-creates the original bridge between earth and sky.[8]

1. Eliade 1964, pp. 346–49; Schnitger 1939, pp. 84–100.

2. See, for example, Becker n.d., p. 13.

3. Giglioli 1893, p. 124.

4. Warneck (1909, pp. 14, 64–66, 93–94) and Winkler (1925, pp. 166–83) discuss various types of magical potions used by the Batak.

5. Nomenclature varies. Personal names in Pichler (n.d.) and Ophuijsen (1911) have been used in this catalogue.

6. See, for example, Pleyte 1894; Pichler n.d.; Ophuijsen 1911; Reschke 1935; Schnitger 1939, pp. 84–100; and Rodgers 1988, p. 208.

7. Ophuijsen 1911.

8. Reschke 1935.

17

Tungkot malehat

North Sumatra (Batak)
19th–20th century
Wood, fiber, feathers
H. 58½ in. (148.6 cm)
Gift of Fred and Rita Richman, 1988
1988.143.90

Exhibited: New York, The Metropolitan
Museum of Art, 1989

Published: Hersey 1991, pl. 5

In addition to the *tunggal panaluan* (no. 16), the *datu* used another type of ritual staff, the *tungkot malehat*. Unlike the former, on which multiple figures were carved directly on the wooden staff, the *tungkot malehat* usually depicts a single figure carved from a separate piece of wood and joined to the shaft. Cast copper alloy figures were sometimes used instead of wooden ones (see no. 18), and a variety of woods, including bamboo and rattan, were employed for the shaft.[1]

It is not clear whether the solitary figure, seen seated, standing, or riding a horse or a *singa*, portrays the twin brother Si Adji Donda Hatahutan, as in the topmost figure on the *tunggal panaluan* staff from which the *tungkot malehat* is thought to derive (see no. 16). The seated figure on this staff wears a plaited fiber headband crowned with feathers. He grasps both knees, a gesture frequently seen in seated figures. The contrast between softly modeled features and sharply rendered limbs lends the image a subtle tension. A fiber sheath of the same construction as the headband covers the area where the rattan shaft and wooden figure are joined together.[2]

1. Some examples have magical formulas inscribed on the shaft, such as one collected in the 1920s by the American anthropologist Fay-Cooper Cole and now in the Field Museum of Natural History, Chicago (acc. no. 161380).

2. Most other examples employ a smaller brass ring at this juncture. The use here of a wider plaited-fiber sheathing recalls another type of staff in which magical substances were deposited inside the fiber covering. The carved figure on such implements, however, usually emerges from within the sheathed portion (for example, Sibeth 1991, p. 129, fig. 155) or below it (for example, Cameron 1985b, p. 94, fig. 90).

18

Figure

North Sumatra (Batak)
19th–20th century
Copper alloy
H. 4½ in. (11.4 cm)
Gift of Fred and Rita Richman, 1988
1988.143.141

Exhibited: New York, The Metropolitan
Museum of Art, 1989

Published: Hersey 1991, p. 31

This kneeling figure is almost certainly the finial of a *tungkot malehat* ritual staff (see also no. 17) rather than a knife or sword handle, as has been suggested elsewhere.[1] Unlike the larger *tunggal panaluan* (such as no. 16), on which several figures are directly carved, the smaller *tungkot malehat* features a single wooden or metal figure that was often carved or cast separately (such as this one) and then joined to a staff of rattan or bamboo. A brass figure similar to this one and still attached to its wooden staff in the collection of the Volkenkundig Museum Nusantara, Delft, strongly suggests that the Metropolitan piece served the same function.[2]

The cast figure has a disproportionately large head crowned by a helmet headdress decorated with bilaterally symmetrical double spirals and a beaded border. He wears a matching beaded torque around his neck and holds a cylindrical vessel on his lap. The figure is hollow, and filled with a dark, hardened substance that was probably added to increase the object's ritual efficacy. The substance is visible through open sections of the headdress and above the cylindrical vessel.

1. Hersey 1991, pp. 30–31.

2. Delft, Volkenkundig Museum Nusantara, 1967, p. 75, no. 333.

19

Naga morsarang

North Sumatra (Batak)
19th–20th century
Water buffalo horn, wood
L. 20½ in. (52.1 cm)
Gift of Fred and Rita Richman, 1987
1987.453.1

Exhibited: New York, The Metropolitan
Museum of Art, 1988b, pp. 224–25,
pl. 16; New York, The Metropolitan
Museum of Art, 1989

Published: Hersey 1980, p. 79

The *datu*, or ritual specialist, required a variety of containers made of different materials for his powerful mixtures and potions. This vessel, a *naga morsarang*, utilizes the hollow horn of the water buffalo, its outer surface incised with curving foliate designs. The horn's pointed end is carved in the form of a seated human figure. The wider, open end is plugged with a wooden stopper that depicts the mythical *singa* with four human figures riding on its back. Some examples represent, in the interior of the horn, the earth deity Boraspati Ni Tano in the form of a lizard, a motif that occurs on other ritual objects such as the priest's divination book (no. 25).[1]

The term *naga morsarang*, which derives from the serpent deity of the underworld, Naga Padoha, reinforces the *singa*'s association with the cosmic serpent. An analogous fusion of *singa* and serpent imagery occurs on Batak houses, on which supporting beams, regarded as the snake's body, are covered with *singa* masks (nos. 14, 15). Both the house beams and *singa* masks, like this container's body and *singa* stopper, are together identified with the serpent deity. The identity of the human figures, on the other hand, is unclear. One interpretation suggests that they represent the succession of ritual masters preceding the *datu* who owned the container.[2] It is also possible that the figures are related to the mythical characters portrayed on other ritual implements used by the *datu* (see nos. 16, 20–25).

1. Sibeth 1991, p. 138.

2. New York, The Metropolitan Museum of Art, 1988b, p. 224.

20

Pupuk Container[1]

North Sumatra (Batak)
19th–20th century
Ceramic, wood
H. 13 1/2 in. (34.4 cm)
Gift of Fred and Rita Richman, 1988
1988.124.2a,b

Exhibited: Dallas, Dallas Museum of
Art, 1982, p. 68, pl. 35; New York,
The Metropolitan Museum of Art,
1988b, p. 226, pl. 17; New York, The
Metropolitan Museum of Art, 1989

Published: Hersey 1980, p. 78; Hersey
1991, pl. 6; New York, The Metropolitan
Museum of Art, 1988a, p. 81

This container consists of an imported ceramic vessel and a locally made wooden stopper. Such containers were used to store *pupuk*, a powerful mixture of organic substances prepared by the *datu*. *Pupuk* was ritually applied to objects and sculpted figures in order to animate them with supernatural forces for purposes of protection or aggression.[2] Ceramic jars containing magical substances associated with the *pangulubalang*, or captive spirit, were probably the most sacred of the *datu*'s ritual paraphernalia before widespread conversion to Christianity.[3] According to the German missionary who baptized the first Batak converts in 1913, the newly converted leaders "burned all their magical instruments, including their most sacred object, the jar containing the *pangulubalang*, the poison from corpses of killed enemies which had formerly been used to destroy other human beings."[4]

The carved wooden stopper depicts a figure mounted on the mythical *singa*. The rider has a disproportionately large head, an elongated torso, and attenuated limbs. He wears a headdress with a graceful double swirl at the back, accentuated by an outline of chevrons that repeat the sweeping curves. The rest of the figure is undecorated, contrasting sharply with the *singa*'s ornately carved body. The sinuous form, reinforced by a rolled tongue and backward curling forelock terminating in a mask that faces the rider, recalls the *singa*'s association with the serpent-dragon, or *naga*.

The equestrian theme is widespread in Indonesia. Among the Batak, the image of the rider is clearly associated with prestige and supernatural power. It often appears on stone sarcophagi, spirit houses, and chiefs' dwellings. On a smaller scale, it occurs on ritual staffs and on the carved wooden stoppers of ceramic containers. The *singa* often takes the body of a horse, the mount and protector of important ancestors and divine beings.[5]

This green-glazed, mold-made *kendi*, or water pot, was manufactured in China's Fukien Province, probably in the southern trading port of Ch'üan-chou. The vessel's fluted body and short, bulbous side spout suggest that it was probably made during the late seventeenth or early eighteenth century. A maker's mark—*fu*, meaning "blessing"—is stamped on the bottom.[6]

Ceramics imported from China, Vietnam, Thailand, and Japan were valued by many indigenous groups in Island Southeast Asia for their rarity, beauty, and durability. They were used as currency and for ritual purposes, and they were interred with deceased persons of high rank. Wooden lids or stoppers and fine basketry sheathing were often added to the precious containers as they were adapted for local use. The exotic origins of the ceramics undoubtedly increased their value and mystique. The imagery of this stopper—the aristocratic figure mounted on a guardian *singa*—further reinforces the elite character of the imported vessel.

1. *Pupuk* containers such as this one are also referred to as *guri-guri* and *buli-buli* (Müller 1893, figs. 183–85; Winkler 1925, p. 176, no. 11; Jakarta 1980–81, pp. 90–91; Marpaung and Rodgers 1988a, p. 196; and Sibeth 1991, figs. 173–79). Because the basis for the differences in terminology is not clear, a more general descriptive title—*pupuk* container—is used here.

2. *Pupuk* was prepared from the remains of a ritually executed human victim. It was

believed that the victim's spirit could then be called upon to perform the *datu*'s bidding.

3. *Pangulubalang* also referred to the potent mixture prepared from the corpse's body fluids, in contrast to the remains used in preparing the *pupuk* (Müller 1893, p. 67; Warneck 1909, pp. 14, 64–66, 93–94; Winkler 1925, pp. 170–71). The term *pangulubalang* is generally used today to refer to protective stone and wooden figures that were animated by ritual application of

the magical substances mentioned above (Marpaung and Rodgers 1988a, p. 196; Marpaung and Rodgers 1988b, p. 198). Sculpted figures are also referred to as *patung pangulubalang*, literally "image [of] *pangulubalang*" (Jakarta 1984–85, passim).

4. Becker n.d., p. 26.

5. Bartlett 1934, pp. 22–26.

6. Identification, date, and provenance of the imported ceramic vessels in nos. 20–24 were determined in consultation with James C. Y. Watt, Brooke Russell Astor Senior Curator in the Department of Asian Art, The Metropolitan Museum of Art, who also translated the Chinese inscription on this *kendi*. Similar vessels are illustrated in Adhyatman 1987, p. 98, no. 137; and Schoffel 1981, p. 68, no. 57.

21

Pupuk Container

North Sumatra (Batak)
19th–early 20th century
Ceramic, wood
H. 7 1/2 in. (19.1 cm)
Gift of Fred and Rita Richman, 1988
1988.143.39

Exhibited: New York, The Metropolitan Museum of Art, 1989

Most wooden stoppers for *pupuk* containers portray an equestrian figure, as does this one. Horses were probably introduced to the Batak area from the west coast or from Aceh, farther north.[1] Because only the elite could afford them, horses were identified with chiefs and ancestors of high rank. Among the Toba Batak, each family group had a sacred horse that was consecrated to one of the three principal deities according to its descent line. A black horse was sacred to the deity Batara Guru, a brown horse to Soripada, and the piebald to Mangalabulan.[2] The horse was also linked symbolically to other important creatures in Batak mythology, such as the serpent-dragon and the lizard. Among the Angkola Batak, for example, a lizard's tail was ritually cut off by a person entitled to own a horse. The mutilated lizard would then be transformed into a horse in its next life.[3] This association may in part explain the reptilian character of the horse on this particular stopper.

Thirteen subsidiary figures support the primary equestrian figure. Like the rider, their identity is not known. It has been suggested that figures on wooden stoppers for *pupuk* containers represent characters from the legend of Si Adji Donda Hatahutan, a myth more closely associated with the *tunggal panaluan* (such as no. 16).[4] Another myth that might explain the meaning of equestrian figures in Batak art is the legend of the man who rode his horse to the shore of Lake Toba. According to the story, the horse suddenly jumped into the water, and both horse and rider drowned and turned to stone. The drowned man's *begu*, or spirit, became a *solobean* (a malevolent type of *sombaon*, or higher spirit), joining others like it in Lake Toba.[5] Still another interpretation suggests that the equestrian figure is the personification of the *pangulubalang*, or captive spirit, whose essence is contained in the vessel.[6]

The equine imagery on the wooden stopper is echoed in the painted horses on the imported container, another prestige item. The blue-and-white ceramic was manufactured for export in the Swatow area of southern China and dates to the late Ming period (late 16th–early 17th century). Miniature jars such as this one were made in China as containers for the export of oil and ointments to Southeast Asia, where they were exchanged for local aromatics such as cloves, camphor, sandalwood, and frankincense.[7]

1. Bartlett 1934, p. 24.

2. Loeb 1935, p. 91.

3. Bartlett 1934, p. 24.

4. Ibid., pp. 23–24.

5. Warneck 1909. The Batak believed that human beings have two spirits, the *tondi* (the soul of one who is still alive) and the *begu* (the spirit that is released when the person dies). Through offerings and rituals performed by the living, the *begu* could be transformed into higher spirits called *sumangot* and *sombaon* (the highest form).

6. Müller 1893, p. 67.

7. Meilink-Roelofsz 1962, p. 14; Harrisson 1979, p. 81; Singapore, Southeast Asian Ceramic Society, 1979, pp. 92–93.

22

Pupuk Container

North Sumatra (Batak)
19th–early 20th century
Ceramic, wood
H. 6½ in. (16.5 cm)
Gift of Fred and Rita Richman, 1988
1988.143.40

Exhibited: New York, The Metropolitan
Museum of Art, 1989

The carved wooden stopper of this *pupuk* container depicts a human figure mounted on a horse with the exaggerated head of a *singa*. The stopper fits into a translucent green jar with molded decoration manufactured in China, probably in the thirteenth or fourteenth century, during the Yuan dynasty. The use of imported Chinese ceramics by the Batak and other Indonesian groups reflects the highly developed trade network that flourished in the region centuries before the arrival of Europeans. Contact between China and Sumatra can be traced back to the seventh century, when the capital of the mercantile empire of Srivijaya was located in the port of Palembang, in southern Sumatra.[1] From various points of entry, imported ceramics such as this one were probably transported farther inland to interior groups such as the Batak, as northeastern ports rivaling earlier ports in the south emerged from the twelfth to the fifteenth century.[2]

1. Coedès 1968, p. 130. Bronson (1979, passim) has recently questioned the nature and location of Srivijaya.

2. Srivijaya's center is believed to have shifted in the thirteenth century farther inland, near the present site of Jambi (southeast of the Batak area). Recent excavations at Kota Cina in Sumatra have yielded large quantities of white and green wares, indicating that this northeastern site was another important trading settlement from the twelfth to the fourteenth century. Yet another northeastern settlement, the port of Pasai, dominated trade in North Sumatra in the fifteenth century (Edwards McKinnon 1975–77, passim; Guy 1986, pp. 20–21, 26–27, 36–38).

23

Pupuk Container

North Sumatra (Batak)
19th–early 20th century
Ceramic, wood
H. 10 in. (25.4 cm)
Gift of Fred and Rita Richman, 1988
1988.143.38

Exhibited: New York, The Metropolitan
Museum of Art, 1989

Having a tripartite composition, this *pupuk* container presents an interesting variation on the equestrian theme.[1] An avian creature combining aspects of the chicken and the hornbill is shown perched on the head of a rider, who is in turn mounted on a horse with the head of the mythical *singa*. Each of the three elements of the composition—bird, human, and *singa*—is associated with one of the three divisions of the cosmos—the upper, middle, and lower, or underworld.

Birds in Batak mythology were often associated with the upper world of the beneficent spirit kingdom. The entire cosmos, with upper and lower worlds united by the middle world of the living, is represented in works that combine a bird motif with the serpent, symbol of the underworld.[2] The symbolic associations of these images, however, were not restricted to only one of the three realms but frequently linked one realm to another. Birds such as the hornbill and the chicken, for example, were also associated with the lower world of the dead.[3] The *singa*, while identified with the serpent of the underworld, also warded off evil, and living human beings of the middle world could make a transition to the other realms through ritual possession or death. Appropriately, the lead inlays that define the horseman's eyes and mouth on this piece not only recall the ritual pouring of molten lead into the human victim's mouth in the process that would transform his spirit into a *pangulubalang*,[4] they also evoke his close association with the supernatural.

The stopper fits into an imported container with crackled glaze of a type known as Sawankhalok ware, named after the kiln site in Thailand where it was made. It was probably manufactured between the fifteenth and the seventeenth century.

1. A similar composition is used in a brass *pupuk* container in the collection of the Field Museum of Natural History, Chicago (acc. no. 161512; Taylor and Aragon 1991, p. 123, fig. III.42).

2. According to the Batak creation myth, the middle world was created after the deity Batara Guru's daughter leaped from the upper world into the sea below to escape from the courtship of the god Mangalabulan. When a swallow informed Batara Guru of his daughter's plight, he sent back with the bird a handful of earth which the swallow set down upon the sea. The lump of earth grew larger and larger, taking the light away from the serpent of the underworld, Naga Padoha, who shoved it away and allowed it to float off on the waters. Batara Guru sent down more earth and a powerful hero (whose coupling with Batara Guru's daughter brought forth the first human beings) to combat the serpent (Loeb 1935, p. 77). Thus began the eternal struggle between the middle world of the living and the underworld of the dead.

3. See, for example, Warneck 1909, pp. 108–9; and Holt 1967, p. 106.

4. See no. 20 for a discussion of the *pangulubalang*.

24

Pupuk Container

North Sumatra (Batak)
Late 19th–early 20th century
Ceramic, wood
H. 12 in. (30.5 cm)
Gift of Fred and Rita Richman, 1988
1988.143.37

Exhibited: New York, The Metropolitan
Museum of Art, 1989

Published: Hersey 1980, p. 71

Several creatures in Batak mythology converge in this avian image with the oversize head of a *singa*. The avian elements derive from the chicken and possibly the hornbill, while the *singa* head links the creature to the water buffalo, serpent-dragon, and horse. The chicken was an important sacrificial animal and figured prominently in many Batak rituals. A carved representation of the chicken, called *manuk-manuk*, was often hung in the home, where rituals were performed before it.[1] The reverence accorded the chicken may have its roots in the Batak concept of an anthropomorphic supreme god who possessed a magical blue chicken in place of a wife. The chicken laid three eggs out of which emerged the gods Batara Guru, Soripada, and Mangalabulan.[2] The symbolism associated with another bird, the hornbill, is said to have converged with that of the horse. After its introduction to Batak society, the horse acquired many of the indigenous hornbill's symbolic functions, such as that of guardian from and guide to the realms of the spirits.[3] The visual coupling of the chicken-hornbill and the *singa*, creatures associated, respectively, with the upper and the lower worlds, can be interpreted as a metaphor for the union of the two realms through the middle world of the living (see also no. 23).

The brown-glazed ceramic container was probably manufactured in southern China or Vietnam between the fourteenth and the sixteenth century. Similar vessels have been found in the Philippines, reflecting the widespread use of imported wares from the Asian mainland among the various groups in Island Southeast Asia.

1. Warneck 1909, pp. 108–13.

2. Loeb 1935, p. 76.

3. Bartlett 1934, pp. 21–26; Holt 1967, p. 106.

25

Pustaha

North Sumatra (Batak)
19th–20th century
Wood, bark, pigment
H. 7³/4 in. (19.7 cm)
Gift of Fred and Rita Richman, 1988
1988.143.133

Published: Hersey 1991, fig. 14

Fertility and protection through supernatural intervention, major themes in the arts of Southeast Asia, are both expressed in this *pustaha*, or Batak divination book. Among the Batak, sickness and death were caused by the abduction of the deceased's soul by a *begu*, a lower kind of ancestral spirit that had not yet attained a higher spiritual form. The *datu* played a crucial role in defending living souls against possession by these unfriendly spirits.[1] In the *pustaha*, he was instructed by his predecessors, whose secrets were herein revealed. The books also contain prescriptions for the preservation and destruction of life, formulas for ritual healing, agricultural procedures, and the names of the earlier *datus*.[2]

The front cover of this *pustaha* depicts a lizard, a motif frequently found on rice granary doors. The reptile was associated with fertility, for the Batak believed that the agricultural deity Boraspati Ni Tano, who lived inside the earth, manifested herself to men in the form of a lizard. Accordingly, lizards were never killed and were given ritual offerings of rice.[3]

1. Eliade 1964, pp. 346–49.

2. Winkler 1925, passim; Junghuhn 1847, p. 272; Voorhoeve n.d.

3. Warneck 1909, pp. 6, 38.

26

Gana-gana

North Sumatra (Batak)
19th–20th century
Wood, fiber, fabric, shell, metal
H. 41 in. (104.1 cm)
Gift of Fred and Rita Richman, 1988
1988.143.6

Exhibited: New York, The Metropolitan
Museum of Art, 1989

Published: Hersey 1991, pl. 9

Generically referred to as *gana-gana*,[1] sculpted wooden figures imbued with supernatural powers also had individual names, such as those collected by the Italian ethnographer Elio Modigliani in the late nineteenth century. Several of the names recorded at the time began with the word *pagar*, a term now generally used to refer to protective figures.[2] These statues were animated by *begu*, a lower form of ancestral spirit. *Begu* possessed great potential for malevolence which, however, could be manipulated to benefit the living. Accordingly, the ritual specialist would entice them to take up residence in the sculptures, thus bringing them under his control. Only *gana-gana* inhabited by the spirits were effective.[3] Many of the figures have separately carved oversize hands shown in a variety of gestures, sometimes suggesting those used in ritual dance. Others stand with knees slightly bent and hands pressed against the stomach or genital area, as does this one.

This figure wears a bundle of fibers on his head and fabric strips ornamented with cowrie shells and brass spirals around his neck. A square hole on his chest formerly contained the potent substance *pupuk* (see no. 20), from which the statue derived its power. The figure's menacing countenance reinforces its apotropaic function of protecting the living by warding off evil.

1. Like the term *pangulubalang*, which even in the early literature was sometimes loosely applied to different types of objects animated by the captive spirit called *pangulubalang* (no. 20, n. 3), the term *gana-gana* was used in late-nineteenth-century accounts to describe a variety of anthropomorphic representations ranging from figurated bullet holders to wooden stoppers and free-standing wooden and stone figures (Müller 1893, pp. 67–70, nos. 185, 192, 195–96; Giglioli 1893, pp. 124–26, figs. 23, 27). It is clear, nevertheless, that *gana-gana* consistently referred to the visible image animated by the invisible *pangulubalang*.

2. Giglioli 1893, pp. 123–24. The individual names assigned to *gana-gana* collected by Modigliani include Pagar Pagnalùppo, Pagar Saitan, and Si Tappi Sinder. For examples of current usage of the term *pagar*, see Cameron 1985b, pp. 87–90, figs. 76–81; and Sibeth 1991, pp. 128–29, fig. 155.

3. Warneck 1909, p. 119.

27

Si gale-gale

North Sumatra (Batak)
19th–20th century
Wood, metal
H. 11¼ in. (28.6 cm)
Gift of Fred and Rita Richman, 1987
1987.453.6

Exhibited: Dallas, Dallas Museum of
Art, 1982, pl. 39; New York, The
Metropolitan Museum of Art, 1988b,
pp. 228–29, pl. 18; New York, The
Metropolitan Museum of Art, 1989

Published: Hersey 1980, p. 79

This head was formerly part of a nearly lifesize puppet called *si gale-gale*.[1] The wooden figures with jointed limbs were mounted on large wheeled platforms on which, weeping, they danced during funerary ceremonies called *papurpur sepata*, held for persons of high rank who had died without offspring. The ritual dispelled the curse of dying childless, and placated the spirit of the deceased so that he would do no harm to the community.[2]

The use of the *si gale-gale* figure is said to have originated from the legend of a childless woman named Nai Manggale, who on her deathbed instructed her husband to have a lifesize image made of herself to be called *si gale-gale* and to have a dirge played before it. Unless this was done, her spirit would not be admitted to the abode of the dead, which would in turn force her to put a curse on her surviving spouse. To avert this misfortune, the *si gale-gale* was created. *Si gale-gale* figures are either male or female, depending on the gender of the deceased.

Among the earliest references to the *si gale-gale* is the German missionary Johannes Warneck's description of the sculpture's use in the early twentieth century. When a rich man died without a surviving son, his relatives held a special feast both to mourn his death and to demonstrate his wealth. For this festival a wooden figure in the likeness of the deceased was commissioned and clothed in traditional costume, with shawl, headdress, and gold jewelry. Mounted on a wheeled platform and manipulated by an elaborate system of strings, the figure danced while the deceased's wife, parents, and brothers danced alongside, weeping. The image was led ceremoniously to the market, where pork, beef, or buffalo meat was distributed among those gathered. After the prescribed period of dancing, the *si gale-gale* was shot and thrown over the village walls. The Batak saying "Wealthy for a moment like a *si gale-gale* figure" thus refers to a rich man with no heirs to care for his spirit in the afterlife.[3]

Surviving examples of *si gale-gale* figures vary in quality, and, already in the early twentieth century, missionaries noted different levels of expertise among carvers of *si gale-gale* figures. A small number of complete figures survive in German, Dutch, and American collections, some with the wheeled platform and strings intact. The Metropolitan's *si gale-gale*, although missing its body and platform, ranks among the finest examples known. Hindu-Javanese influences are evident in the finely sculpted nose and delicate mouth, which curves in a half smile. Curling eyebrows are of inlaid water buffalo horn, while the hauntingly lifelike, movable eyes are made of an unusual alloy of lead and antimony and have pupils of resin.[4] The brass ear ornaments are of the type called *sitepal*,[5] which are worn by both men and women, making it difficult to ascertain the gender intended. A cavity accessible from the top and back of the head may have held a moist ball of moss or a sponge to enable the figure to weep. A small stick, probably meant to manipulate a movable tongue, is concealed behind the mouth.

1. The confusion between the names *si gale-gale* and *mejan*, both of which have been used to refer to this head, may have resulted from Schnitger's (1939, pp. 103–5) ambiguous reference to a *tukang mejan* (*mejan* carver) rather than to a *tukang si gale-gale* (*si gale-gale* carver).

2. Ibid.

3. Warneck 1909, p. 108.

4. Materials analysis was conducted by Richard E. Stone, Conservator, and Mark T. Wypyski, Assistant Research Scientist, of the Objects Conservation Department, The Metropolitan Museum of Art.

5. Wealthy persons owned this type of earring, called *sitepal* (Amsterdam, Tropenmuseum, 1987, no. 203) or *simanjomak* (Rodgers 1985, nos. 19, 20).

28

Si gale-gale

North Sumatra (Batak)
19th–20th century
Wood, fabric, metal
H. 21½ in. (54.6 cm)
Gift of Fred and Rita Richman, 1988
1988.143.47

Exhibited: New York, The Metropolitan
Museum of Art, 1989

Published: Hersey 1991, pl. 10

Except for its diminutive size, this puppet has all the characteristics of the lifesize *si gale-gale* figure (no. 27); even smaller *si gale-gale* puppets are known to exist, such as the fully clothed example mounted on a wheeled platform collected by the American anthropologist Fay-Cooper Cole in the early twentieth century.[1] It is also possible, however, that this puppet is an example of the smaller figures that accompanied the larger puppets during *si gale-gale* funerary rituals.[2]

The head of this smaller image, like the larger *si gale-gale*, has a cavity accessible from the top and back of the head. The head and limbs are movable to enable the image to dance during the *si gale-gale* ceremony, when it would have been fully clothed.

1. Field Museum of Natural History, Chicago, acc. no. 161453.

2. Schnitger 1939, pp. 103–5, pl. 10. See also Amsterdam, Tropenmuseum, 1987, nos. 41, 42, for examples of figures that are perhaps the precursors of the *si gale-gale* puppets.

A fully clothed *si gale-gale* mounted on a wheeled platform performs to the accompaniment of a musical ensemble. Photograph, before 1941

29

Figure

North Sumatra (Batak)
19th–20th century
Wood
H. 7 in. (17.8 cm)
Gift of Fred and Rita Richman, 1988
1988.143.111

30

Musical Instrument

North Sumatra (Batak)
19th–20th century
Wood
H. 28 in. (71.1 cm)
Gift of Fred and Rita Richman, 1988
1988.143.50

Exhibited: New York, The Metropolitan
Museum of Art, 1989

Another major motif in Batak art is the seated or kneeling figure. The seated figure with arms hugging flexed legs (no. 29) was originally part of a stringed musical instrument called, by the Toba Batak, *hasapi* or, by the Karo Batak, *kulcapi*. Such an instrument is shown here in its entirety, with a kneeling figure whose hands rest on his knees (no. 30).

Linguistic and formal affinities pertaining to similar forms in different parts of Island Southeast Asia are another indicator of close cultural relations between various groups. Similar musical instruments, for example, are called *kutyapi* in Java and *kudyapi* in the southern Philippines, and the motif of the seated human figure, like the instrument itself, also occurs among several different groups.

Although music was nearly always performed by the Batak in a ritual context in former times, widespread conversion to Christianity, which put an end to many traditional rituals in the early decades of the twentieth century, transformed music into the largely secular art form that it is today.

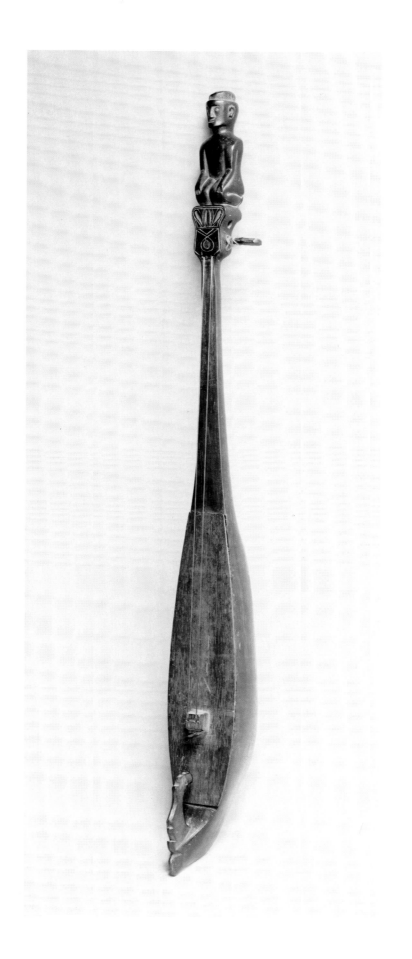

Renowned for their skill in warfare, the Batak used a stunning array of weapons, including several kinds of swords and knives. Swords of this type, called *piso sanalenggam*, are usually associated with Toba and Pakpak Batak groups. This example has a single-edged metal blade and a handle of water buffalo horn finely carved in the shape of a human figure. Because of the frequency of feuds among different Batak groups, the manufacture of metal blades was in former times the blacksmith's most important task.[1] Handles appear to have been carved by other specialists.

Conforming to the horn's natural curve, the kneeling figure tilts slightly forward, his attenuated arms embracing bent knees. The smoothness of the front surface contrasts sharply with the textured back richly decorated in low-relief geometric and foliate patterns. The elegant beauty of this weapon enhanced and reaffirmed the status of its owner.

1. Late-nineteenth- to early-twentieth-century examples of *piso sanalenggam* are documented as having iron blades (Leiden, Rijksmuseum voor Volkenkunde, 1914, p. 103, nos. 1239/253, 254). More recent documentation describes Batak swords as having steel blades manufactured by the welding together of thin strips of steel (Sibeth 1991, pp. 166–68), undoubtedly a later development. The metal from which this blade is made appears to be iron, although a materials analysis has not yet been made.

32

Parpanggalahan

North Sumatra (Batak)
19th–20th century
Water buffalo horn, wood
H. 7¼ in. (18.4 cm)
Gift of Fred and Rita Richman, 1988
1988.143.139

Exhibited: New York, The Metropolitan
Museum of Art, 1989

The Batak were skilled in the use of a wide assortment of bladed weapons and firearms. Gunpowder was manufactured from a local supply of sulfur, which was melted down and mixed with powdered charcoal, saltpeter, and lime extract. To increase its efficacy, shredded leaves gathered during a thunderstorm and herbs harvested during an earthquake and then stored for future use were added to the concoction. This ensured that the mixture would have the destructive power of an earthquake and of thunder.[1] The powder was stored inside the house in large gourds.[2] The chief carried his own personal supply in a carved water buffalo horn container such as this one, which he wore suspended from a chain around his neck.

The outside surface of the horn is carved with curvilinear motifs also seen on architectural carvings. A frontal *singa* mask, to which a suspension chain would have been attached, protrudes at the center. The *singa*, symbolizing power, protection, and prestige, is represented in other Batak art forms such as carved wooden stoppers for *pupuk* containers (nos. 20, 22–24) and on a larger scale in architectural carvings (nos. 14, 15).

1. Brenner 1894, p. 290.

2. Giglioli 1893, p. 122.

33

Figure

North Sumatra (Batak)
19th–20th century
Wood
H. 6³/4 in. (17.2 cm)
Gift of Fred and Rita Richman, 1988
1988.143.113

Exhibited: New York, The Metropolitan
Museum of Art, 1989

This wooden implement, which depicts a standing human figure holding a vessel with both hands, is almost certainly a ritual lime squeezer.[1] The Batak used lime in a number of ceremonial contexts. It was, for example, mixed with water and used in the ceremonial cleansing of a horse about to be consecrated to one of the three principal deities, Batara Guru, Soripada, and Mangalabulan (see no. 21). The citrus juice was also added to various mixtures such as magic potions and gunpowder to improve their efficacy.[2] And in rituals designed to foretell the future, lime segments would be used, together with chicken eggs, by the *datu*.[3]

1. This object has previously been described as a ritual planting stick. Its size and shape, however, strongly suggest that it was used for extracting lime juice. Similar lime implements are documented in Sibeth (1991, p. 147, fig. 181). Early German texts (for example, Warneck 1909, p. 44; and Brenner 1894, p. 220) use the word *citrone* (lemon), but the local citrus fruit is really a kind of lime. Limes were not yet well known in the West in the nineteenth century, hence the misnomer.

2. See, for example, Brenner 1894, p. 290.

3. Warneck 1909, pp. 110–13.

34

Headddress

West Sumatra (Minangkabau)
19th–20th century
Wood, gold leaf
L. 10¼ in. (26 cm)
Gift of Fred and Rita Richman, 1988
1988.143.120

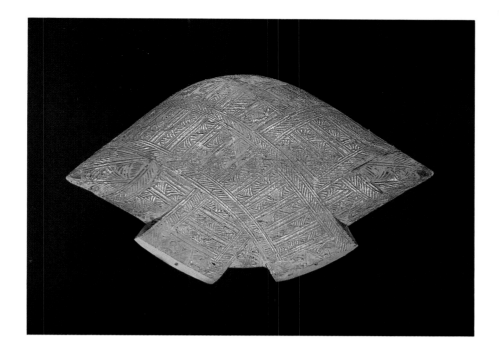

This gilt headdress is an elegant rendition of the double buffalo horn motif that dominates the art and architecture of the Minangkabau people of West Sumatra. Replicating the *tengkuluak* headcloth, which was wrapped around the head to form a horn on each side, this wooden ornament re-creates, in carved relief, woven textile motifs. Gilding effectively evokes the splendor of the gold supplementary weft threads in the cloth versions. Triangular motifs on the border of each of the overlapping ends (see detail) depict the *pucuak rabuang*, or bamboo shoot, a prominent motif on both carved objects and woven textiles associated with the notion of strength that springs from within.[1]

This headdress was probably part of a Minangkabau bride's dowry, which included different kinds of gold headdresses, precious silk-and-gold *kain songket* textiles, gold bracelets, rings, earrings, pectorals, and ornate repoussé buckles.[2] The headgear repeats the configuration of the curving roofs of traditional houses, which are said to commemorate the legendary victory of the Minangkabau calf over a mighty Javanese bull in a combat that won for the Minangkabau their freedom from the invading Javanese, the upward sweep of the roofs representing the horns of the defeated bull.[3] The head ornament's shape is also associated with the primordial mother, Bundo Kanduang, after whom the Minangkabau costume that features the *tengkuluak* headcloth is named.[4] Concepts of ethnic identity and the ideal woman-mother are thus encoded in the shape of the headdress.

1. The *pucuak rabuang* clearly derives from the *tumpal* motif used in silk patola cloths from India, which were traded throughout Southeast Asia. The multiple meanings associated with the bamboo shoot are discussed in Kartiwa 1984, pp. 70–71. Formal variations on the motif are demonstrated in Ramli 1978.

2. Maass 1910, pp. 423–28.

3. The curved roof is also said to represent the ship that landed on top of the sacred mountain, Merapi, bringing the first Minangkabau people to the area (Capistrano-Baker n.d.). Errington (1984, pp. 83–112) observes that the Minangkabau often attribute several different meanings to the same form.

4. Kartiwa 1984, pp. 42–43; Kartiwa 1986, pp. 25–26.

35

Gelang gadang polang

West Sumatra (Minangkabau)
19th–20th century
Wood, metal, gold leaf
Diam. 5³/4 in. (14.6 cm)
Gift of Fred and Rita Richman, 1988
1988.143.121

Among the Minangkabau people of West Sumatra, bracelets were traditionally worn only by young girls. Mothers handed down their armbands to their daughters when they were about nine years old.[1] The thick bangles, called *gelang gadang polang*, were always worn in pairs, one on each arm. Elaborate bracelets such as this one were worn at weddings and other special occasions.[2] The bracelet's carved outer surface is gilt, the plain inner surface lined with a smooth metal sheet.

According to the Minangkabau, meanings are encoded in all carving and weaving motifs, though many are no longer remembered.[3] Motifs still known today include the lozenge-shaped *saik galamai* and the crescent-shaped *kuku*, seen here on the back and border (see detail). *Saik galamai* is a ceremonial cake; cut into lozenge-shaped servings, it alludes to the importance of cooperation, as several people are needed to help in its preparation.[4] The *kuku*, or fingernail motif, by contrast, serves as a reminder to treat others as oneself: one should dig one's nails into one's own skin, and feel the pain, before doing the same to another.[5]

1. Maass 1910, p. 264.

2. Delft, Volkenkundig Museum Nusantara, 1984, pp. 48–51.

3. Recent studies that focus on Minangkabau textile designs and their meanings include Kartiwa 1984; Kartiwa 1986; Ng 1987; and Summerfield and Summerfield 1991. Carving motifs are discussed in Capistrano-Baker n.d.

4. Kartiwa 1984, pp. 73–74.

5. Interview with master carver Fauzi Sutan Pado Manggih in the village of Pandai Sikek, West Sumatra, 1991 (Capistrano-Baker n.d.). In a recent study of the social function of Minangkabau textiles, Ng (1987, p. 244) documents a similar weaving motif from the village of Nagari Koto nan Gadang as a *pucuak rabuang*, or bamboo shoot, a motif more frequently rendered in a triangular configuration throughout the Minangkabau region.

A group of Minangkabau men and young women. The women wear carved wooden headdresses and large *gelang gadang polang* bracelets. Print made after a photograph, from the reports of the Rheinische Missionsgesellschaft (March 1874)

36

Besihung

Lampung
19th–20th century
Iron
L. 18½ in. (47 cm)
Gift of Fred and Rita Richman, 1988
1988.143.172

One important social ritual in the Lampung region in southern Sumatra was the filing and blackening of teeth at puberty to indicate the attainment of marriageable age. Soot from burned twigs to be used for blackening the teeth was collected in *besihung*, forged iron containers in the shape of a water buffalo, cock, deer, or proa, a kind of Malayan sailboat. This example, in a symmetrical ship configuration, represents a female container. In contrast, male containers are asymmetrical.[1]

The practice of blackening the teeth, which ended at the beginning of this century, was originally associated with the supernatural. Like other important occasions, teeth filing was accompanied by ritual feasting. The metal container, whose various forms were associated with supernatural forces, was oriented toward the river and moved downstream during the ceremony.[2] The boat shape recalls textile motifs in the well-known *tampan* and *pelapai*, ceremonial cloths that were used in important rites of passage including circumcision, marriage, and death.[3] The use of ship imagery in both *besihung* and ritual textiles recapitulates the transitional aspect of the events in which they were used.[4]

1. *Besihung* are also known as *pelaloan* and *tinggang* (Amsterdam, Tropenmuseum, 1987, p. 278, no. 272; Palm 1965, pp. 67–72).

2. Delft, Volkenkundig Museum Nusantara, 1984, pp. 13–14; Palm 1965, p. 68.

3. Steinmann 1965b, pp. 25–26; Gittinger 1972; Maxwell 1990, p. 113.

4. Ship imagery in Indonesian art is discussed further in Steinmann 1965a and Steinmann 1965b.

37

Siraha salawa

Nias
19th–20th century
Wood
H. 25 in. (63.5 cm)
Gift of Fred and Rita Richman, 1987
1987.453.3

Exhibited: New York, The Metropolitan
Museum of Art, 1989

Published: Hersey 1980, p. 74

This seated male figure resembles those generally thought to be from northern Nias. The highly prestigious image, called *siraha salawa*, represents a distant or founding ancestor whose function was to protect the house of a nobleman.[1] Although Nias households had numerous smaller ancestor figures called *adu zatua*, each house had only one *siraha salawa*, which was erected inside on a free-standing post.[2] Like most such figures, this *siraha salawa* sits on a low stool, holding a cup with both hands.[3] He wears personal accouterments restricted to male nobility, namely the high, peaked crown *ni'o wöli wöli*, the necklace *kalabubu*, a moustachelike face ornament, one ear pendant, and an armband.[4]

Three carving styles have been identified on the island of Nias, corresponding to three geographic divisions, namely, north, central, and south. There is, however, some ambiguity in the literature regarding regional characteristics. For example, the W configuration formed by the arms and hands holding the cup is said to be characteristic of all northern Nias images.[5] Early German documentation, however, describes a similarly seated figure holding a cup in the same distinctive configuration as an example of a major form that was especially widespread in southern Nias.[6] To cite a second example, another gesture, of one hand holding a cup and the other a betel-nut crusher, is said to be unique to southern Nias,[7] although a seated figure in Cologne depicting this gesture has a northern Nias provenance.[8] Information regarding these figures along with numerous early examples unfortunately disappeared as the people of Nias converted to Christianity and renounced traditional beliefs, leaving ambiguities and contradictions in our understanding of traditional art forms today.

1. The term *siraha* generally refers to protective figures throughout Nias, while *salawa* means "chief" in northern Nias (Feldman 1985, pp. 48–51).

2. Basel, Museum für Völkerkunde, 1930, p. 9.

3. The stool is not articulated in this piece but merely suggested, by two low posts that support the figure in back.

4. Delft, Volkenkundig Museum Nusantara, 1990, pl. 29; Schröder 1917, pl. 8: fig. 16; pl. 21: figs. 48, 49; Wirz 1929, pls. 6, 7.

5. Feldman 1985, p. 48; Feldman 1990, p. 32.

6. Horsky 1942, pp. 378–79, pl. 23, fig. 1.

7. Feldman 1985, p. 67; Feldman 1990, p. 34.

8. Delft, Volkenkundig Museum Nusantara, 1990, p. 200, no. 22.

38

Adu zatua

Nias
19th–20th century
Wood
H. 14 in. (35.6 cm)
Gift of Fred and Rita Richman, 1988
1988.143.64

Exhibited: New York, The Metropolitan
Museum of Art, 1989

The people of Nias believed that the spirits of the dead possessed supernatural powers and were capable of influencing the living in a positive or a negative way. They thus sought to appease and influence them by honoring *adu zatua*, wooden images carved in their likeness.[1]

Such images were made shortly after an individual's death. When the sculpture was finished, the departed spirit was encouraged to inhabit the figure through ceremonies performed by a ritual specialist, who then informed the dead person's oldest son that his parent had returned to the house. Although *adu zatua* were collectively owned by all descendants of the deceased,[2] it was this son's responsibility to ensure that the image was properly nourished with ritual offerings of food.[3] *Adu zatua* were usually lashed to the right wall of the main room of the house. Another figure would be added each time a member of the household died.[4]

Female *adu zatua* such as this one wear a pair of earrings and armbands, in contrast to the single ear pendant and armband worn by male figures. Holding a peg in each hand, this figure also wears a necklace and a smaller, modified version of the nobleman's fernlike, peaked headdress.[5] The higher the rank of the deceased for whom the figure was carved, the more the *adu zatua* image resembled the prestigious *siraha salawa* (no. 37) in quality and elaboration. This figure's posture, with slightly bent knees and solidly rendered calves, suggests a central Nias provenance.[6]

1. Horsky 1942, pp. 378–79.

2. Ibid., p. 383.

3. Wuppertal-Barmen, Vereinigte Evangelische Mission, n.d., pp. 23–24.

4. Feldman 1985, pp. 51–52. A parallel may be drawn with *korwar* figures (no. 45) from Cenderawasih Bay. Like *adu zatua*, a new figure would be added to the household altar after each death and consulted before important undertakings.

5. Delft, Volkenkundig Museum Nusantara, 1990; Schröder 1917, pl. 12: fig. 24.

6. Feldman 1985, pp. 51, 54–59; Feldman 1990, pp. 24–31; and Delft, Volkenkundig Museum Nusantara, 1990.

39

Adu zatua

Nias
19th–20th century
Wood
H. 14³/₄ in. (37.5 cm)
Gift of Fred and Rita Richman, 1988
1988.143.65

Exhibited: New York, The Metropolitan
Museum of Art, 1989

Published: Hersey 1991, fig. 25

On the island of Nias, spirits of deceased ancestors continued to concern them-selves with the daily affairs of the living. They would thus be consulted before any important undertaking through the medium of *adu zatua* figures such as this one. This stylized figure has an attenuated torso and stumps in place of arms. The *ni'o wöli wöli* headdress, with the distinctive double spiral and the abbreviated arms, is characteristic of many *adu zatua* attributed to southern Nias.[1] The figure wears an open jacket and a beardlike chin ornament, clothing and personal ornamentation typically worn by Nias warriors.

1. Delft, Volkenkundig Museum Nusantara,
1990; Feldman 1985, pp. 60–74.

40

Hazi nuwu

Nias (probably Batu Islands)
19th–20th century
Wood, bamboo, rattan
H. 13 1/2 in. (34.3 cm)
Gift of Fred and Rita Richman, 1988
1988.143.63

Exhibited: New York, The Metropolitan
Museum of Art, 1989

Published: Hersey 1980, p. 82

Wooden images such as this one, carved to commemorate the dead, served as the medium through which the soul returned to the world of the living.[1] Geometric planes and volumes articulate this figure's features in a style that suggests a provenance from the Batu Islands, where *adu zatua* images are called *hazi nuwu*. More abstracted than the *adu zatua* figures from the main island of Nias, *hazi nuwu* are usually without arms and rendered with a minimum of detail. The *famaso*, or bamboo tube filled with small sticks that is tied to this effigy, was the receptacle through which the soul entered the figure.[2] According to nineteenth-century accounts, the deceased's soul entered a spider, which was then placed in the bamboo container.[3] According to another source, the dying person's last breath was captured in the bamboo tube before it was attached to the figure.[4]

1. The people of Nias believed that man was made of three elements: the material body, breath (the essence of life), and the soul. The soul, which the living sought to influence, remained after death (Marschall 1982, p. 23).

2. Feldman 1990, pp. 34–35; Delft, Volkenkundig Museum Nusantara, 1990.

3. Summarized in Feldman 1985, p. 52; Feldman 1990, pp. 32–33; and Marschall 1982, p. 23.

4. Feldman 1985, p. 52; Feldman 1990, p. 33.

41

Kareau

Nicobar Islands
19th–20th century
Wood
H. 32 in. (81.3 cm)
Gift of Fred and Rita Richman, 1988
1988.143.96

Exhibited: New York, The Metropolitan
Museum of Art, 1989

The Nicobarese believed in spirits called *iwi* who caused sickness or death unless they were propitiated or frightened away.[1] Accordingly, protective *kareau* figures were placed at house entrances or interiors to banish the malevolent spirits.[2] Such guardians normally depict humans or sometimes animals in threatening poses.[3] The male figure is usually portrayed brandishing a sword or spear. The more menacing the figure's countenance, the more efficacious it was thought to be. Greater protective powers were attributed to female than to male *kareau* because they could detect the *iwi*'s evil intentions earlier and were thus able to forewarn those involved.[4]

This male *kareau* is poised to strike with his spear. The posture, with one arm outstretched and the other bent, is similar to that of other such figures brought to Europe in the late nineteenth century.[5] Originally, the figure probably wore a fabric loincloth. Hanging strips of colored cloth or shell ornaments may have been tied to the wrists and perhaps adorned the pierced ears. Relief carving and black paint articulate the hairline. The figure's aggressive pose is reinforced by bulging eyes of mother-of-pearl with protruding black pupils fixed in a piercing gaze.

1. Man 1889, p. 368.

2. Such figures are sometimes referred to as "soul catchers." This is inaccurate, for they were meant not to catch but rather to scare away evil spirits (Svoboda 1893, p. 14; Man 1882, p. 277). The confusion may stem from the healing methods reportedly used by medicine men in Car Nicobar, which included rescuing the soul abducted by malevolent spirits (Eliade 1964, p. 343).

3. "Die *Kareau* sind Schnitzwerke aus weichem Holze, seltener aus hartem Holze oder Thon erzeugt, welche zumeist menschliche Gestalten, seltener Thiere darstellen, und den Zweck haben, den bösen Geist zu schrecken, zu verscheuchen." (Svoboda 1893, p. 14).

4. Ibid.

5. Similar figures are published in Man 1882, pl. 25; Man n.d., pl. 14; and Svoboda 1893, pl. 2.

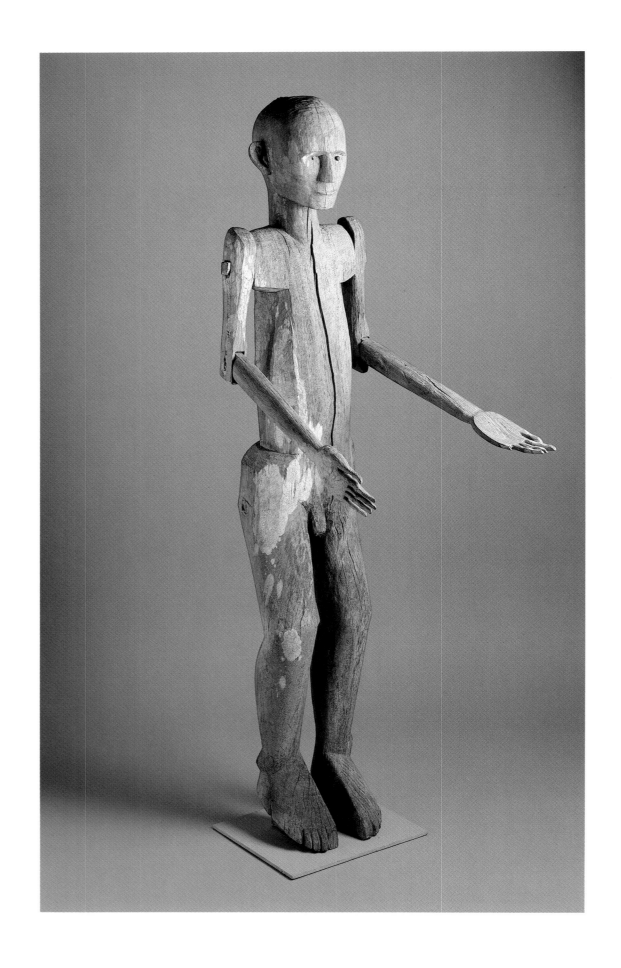

42

Tau-tau

South Sulawesi (Sa'dan Toraja)[1]
19th–20th century
Wood
H. 47½ in. (120.7 cm)
Gift of Fred and Rita Richman, 1988
1988.143.91

Exhibited: New York, The Metropolitan
Museum of Art, 1989

Published: Hersey 1991, pl. 22

The Toraja people on the island of Sulawesi carved lifesize images called *tau-tau* for use in funerary rituals held for high-ranking individuals. Unlike most other types of ancestor figures in Southeast Asia, the *tau-tau* functioned more as a portrait of the deceased than as a receptacle for the soul;[2] it also ensured that the dead person's descendants would long remember his name and accomplishments. The soul itself resided in the spirit world, surrounded by the pigs and water buffalos that had been sacrificed at his funeral.[3]

The wood used to create the *tau-tau* was from the *nangka*, or jackfruit tree, which was harvested according to prescribed procedures. First, the tree was felled while still alive. Initially lemon yellow, the harvested wood acquired a deep brown color similar to that of Toraja skin after several weeks of lubrication with coconut oil. The figure's head was carved from the top of the trunk and the feet were carved from the bottom. Each stage of the carving process was accompanied by ritual offerings, culminating in the slaughter of pigs when the sculpture was finished. Consecrated with prayers and clothed in garments appropriate to the status of the deceased, the *tau-tau* then became a *bombo di kita*, a "soul that is seen"; it also served as a silent reminder that the requisite seven-day feast to commemorate the death of an important person, of which the creation of the *tau-tau* was an integral part, had been held.[4]

1. "Toraja," a generic term used by outsiders to refer to the indigenous people of Sulawesi, has come to be more specifically associated with the people of the Sa'dan Valley, in the south, peoples in the north having rejected the designation, identifying themselves instead according to their ethnic group (Kaudern 1944, pp. 1–3; Aragon 1991, pp. 173–75).

2. Aragon 1991, p. 177. This interpretation, given by contemporary Toraja Christians, is probably influenced by Christian doctrine, which forbids the worship of gods and spirits. The identification of the *tau-tau* ("like a person") with the soul is evident in the use of the term *bombo di kita* ("soul that is seen") to refer to the wooden effigy (Crystal 1985, pp. 131–41).

3. Crystal 1985, p. 140.

4. Ibid., pp. 131–40.

43

Sanggori

Central Sulawesi
19th–20th century
Metal alloy
H. 8 in. (20.3 cm)
Gift of Fred and Rita Richman, 1988
1988.143.117

Published: Hersey 1991, fig. 38

A spiral-shaped head ornament resembling a coiled serpentine creature, the *sanggori* was used in different ways and known by various names among several groups in Sulawesi. In all cases, however, the ornament was worn solely by men.[1] The coiled image has been compared both to the *naga* and to the eel,[2] its spiral shape related to that of ornaments found farther north made from wild boar tusks.[3]

In east Central Sulawesi during festivals honoring the dead, *sanggori* were worn held in place by means of a cloth wrapped around the head, with the tail pointing to the right.[4] The *sanggori* was also an important element of mortuary sculpture. The carved wooden *pemia* head, which was then fastened to the bone bundle of a deceased aristocrat during secondary burial, always had such an ornament attached to it through a perforated projection on the crown.[5] In other parts of Central Sulawesi, priests wore the ornament during healing rituals, on the left side of the head with the tail pointing to the front.[6] *Sanggori* were also among the ritual offerings used in ceremonies to bring forth rain during prolonged periods of dry weather.[7]

1. Kaudern (1944, pp. 321–23) reports that this type of ornament was called *balalao-engki* in northwest Central Sulawesi, *sanggori* in east Central Sulawesi, and *soelang* in north and northeast Sulawesi.

2. Ibid., pp. 320–21.

3. Ibid., pp. 327–32. The prerogative of the head warrior, such ornaments, called *soelang*, were made either of brass or from the upper and lower tusks of a wild boar. The upper tusk was believed to symbolize a shield and the lower tusk, a sword.

4. Ibid., pp. 326–27, fig. 218.

5. Adriani and Kruyt 1912–14, cited in Kaudern 1944, p. 325. Secondary burial, in which cleaned bones were reburied after the flesh had decomposed, was practiced in many parts of Southeast Asia.

6. Sarasin and Sarasin 1905, vol. 2, p. 70.

7. Hissink 1912, cited in Kaudern 1944, p. 323. Other objects offered during such a ceremony included a shield, a sword, a helmet, and the distinctive *taiganja* ear ornament.

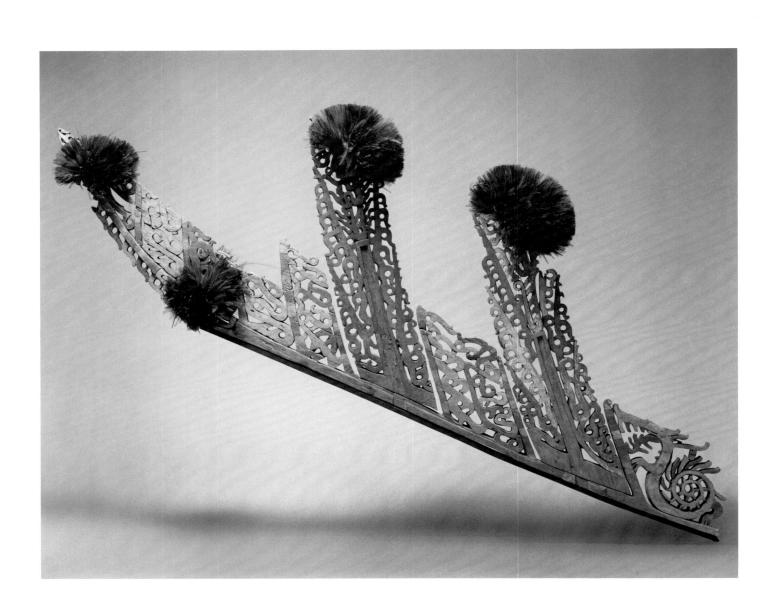

44

Canoe Prow

Irian Jaya (Cenderawasih Bay)
19th–20th century
Wood, cassowary feathers, pigment
L. 58 in. (147.3 cm)
Gift of Fred and Rita Richman, 1988
1988.143.82

Exhibited: New York, The Metropolitan
Museum of Art, 1989

Surrounded by oceans and connected inland by rivers, the people of Island South-east Asia depended on sailing vessels for transportation and communication. This ornate openwork prow from Cenderawasih Bay was formerly part of a seagoing canoe. Such vessels were normally twenty-five feet or more in length, hollowed out of a single log, with two outriggers and two masts and a thatched deckhouse in between.[1] The prow's elaborate fretwork incorporates four anthropomorphic images, one on each of the three raked projections and one on the front base. Each figure, rendered in the *korwar* style (see no. 45), is embellished with a spray of cassowary feathers, creating a fluffy head of hair that would have rustled in the wind as the canoe sailed out to sea. The openwork curvilinear motifs are ordered in clearly defined registers, a characteristic seen in other Cenderawasih Bay art, such as bamboo lime containers.

1. Powell (1958, pp. 112–15) describes the construction of outrigger canoes. Held (1957, fig. 31, opposite p. 132) provides a rare illustration of a similar prow still attached to its canoe.

45

Korwar

Irian Jaya (Cenderawasih Bay)
19th–20th century
Wood, beads, pigment
H. 11 in. (27.9 cm)
Gift of Fred and Rita Richman, 1988
1988.143.45

Exhibited: New York, The Metropolitan
Museum of Art, 1989

Ancestor figures such as this one are called *korwar*, a term that refers to the spirit of the deceased and, by extension, to the wooden image made in its likeness.[1] The position of the seated figure, with elbows resting on drawn-up knees and two hands under the chin, is similar to that of a monumental funerary figure from Vietnam (no. 58) and of a diminutive squatting image from Northern Luzon (no. 60). Stylistic markers, such as the distinctive arrow-shaped nose and abstracted limbs with hands rendered as simply rounded elements, distinguish this image from other renditions of related themes elsewhere in Island Southeast Asia. The similarity of the so-called *korwar* style to other art styles has raised many intriguing questions regarding linguistic and cultural affinities in the region.[2] This figure wears a conical headdress with petallike segments neatly arranged around the top of a disproportionately large head.[3]

Carved shortly after the death of a high-ranking individual, the *korwar* served as a link between the living and the dead. It was manufactured according to prescribed ritual and placed in the family house, where it served as a seat for the deceased's spirit which was then called upon to inhabit the figure. The *korwar* was honored with ritual offerings and consulted before any important undertaking, such as a war expedition or an extended fishing trip. If the *korwar*'s advice proved wrong, the family might intentionally damage or destroy the figure. Old *korwar*, particularly those of lesser-ranking ancestors, were transferred after several years to cliff burials to make room for new images carved for the more recently deceased.[4]

1. Baaren 1968, p. 85.

2. The question of whether Cenderawasih Bay cultures are linguistically and culturally Melanesian or Austronesian is discussed in Held 1957, pp. 1–8.

3. In this, it closely resembles a slightly larger version said to date to the early twentieth century in the collection of the Volkenkundig Museum Nusantara, Delft (Hoog 1959, fig. 10). It has been suggested that the exaggerated head may have evolved from the practice of incorporating the deceased's skull in the small wooden figure. See, for example, Baaren 1968, pls. 1–5.

4. Solheim 1985, pp. 150–51.

46

Iene

Southeast Moluccas, Leti style[1]
19th–20th century
Wood
H. 9 in. (22.9 cm)
Gift of Fred and Rita Richman, 1988
1988.143.105

Exhibited: New York, The Metropolitan
Museum of Art, 1989

On Leti and its neighboring islands in Southeast Moluccas, seated images called *iene* were carved shortly after a person's death to serve as a receptacle for the departed spirit. Like the *korwar* figures of Cenderawasih Bay (no. 45), *iene* are usually shown seated or squatting, with knees drawn up to the chest and elbows resting on the knees. Those in the Leti style often have arms folded across the top of the knees. This example, though eroded, is clearly related to no. 48, particularly in the rendering of the torso and limbs. Its weathered surface suggests that it may have been used as part of an outdoor altar. Honored with offerings of food and prayers,[2] *iene*, like *korwar*, bridged the spirit world and the realm of the living.

1. It is difficult to ascertain the specific islands of origin for *iene* figures whose provenance was not documented at the time they were collected. The stylistic attribution used here is based on Hoog's (1959) classification of anthropomorphic representations from Southeast Moluccas into three major styles, namely the Tanimbar, Babar, and Leti. He defines the last as being characterized by a more delicate finish than that from the other island groups. He further distinguishes two substyles within the Leti style, the Lakor and the Damar.

2. Riedel 1886, pl. 37, reprinted in New York, The Metropolitan Museum of Art, 1988b, p. 316, pl. 62.

47

Iene

Southeast Moluccas, probably Kai
Islands, Leti style
19th century
Wood
H. 22³/₄ in. (57.8 cm)
Gift of Fred and Rita Richman, 1988
1988.143.102

Ex collection: Museum für Völkerkunde, Berlin

Exhibited: New York, The Metropolitan
Museum of Art, 1988b, p. 318,
pl. 63; New York, The Metropolitan
Museum of Art, 1989

Published: Hersey 1980, p. 74; Hersey
1991, fig. 47

This male *iene* sits on a low four-legged stool with folded arms resting on bent knees in a posture widely seen throughout Island Southeast Asia. The tapered head ornament recalls the topknot on seated figures from Vietnam (no. 58) and the Philippines (no. 60), and the more elaborate headdresses on those from Borneo (no. 1) and Cenderawasih Bay (no. 45). It has been suggested that such ornaments may indicate the status of the individual portrayed.[1]

The pedestal and stool on which the figure is enthroned indicate that the sculpture represents a high-ranking individual, probably an important clan ancestor or a village founder. The distinctive grain of the wood is characteristic of the *Cordia subcordata Lamk.*, a sacred tree frequently used for representations of important deities and protective spirits. Images of village founders were sometimes identified with the supreme male god of heaven, Upulere.[2]

1. New York, The Metropolitan Museum of Art, 1988b, p. 316, pl. 62.

2. Amsterdam, Tropenmuseum, 1987, p. 271, no. 146. At annual religious festivals, the people of Leti celebrated the sexual union of the male and female principles personified by the male sun god, Upulere, and the female earth goddess, Upunusa, because their coition produced rain needed for agricultural growth (Taylor and Aragon 1991, p. 233). Hoog (1959, p. 85, nos. 32, 37, figs. 37, 41) proposes that two figures similar to this one in the Rijksmuseum voor Volkenkunde, Leiden, represent the god Upulere.

48

Iene

Southeast Moluccas, Leti style
19th–20th century
Wood
H. 13³/₄ in. (34.9 cm)
Gift of Fred and Rita Richman, 1987
1987.453.5

Exhibited: New York, The Metropolitan
Museum of Art, 1988b, pl. 62

Published: Hersey 1980, p. 83

The finely carved head and the ear ornaments that adorn this figure indicate that it represents an important individual, probably a high-ranking ancestor whose spirit resided in the wooden image. According to late-nineteenth-century literature, such sculptures were carved by a ritual specialist five days after a person's death, when the departed spirit would inhabit the figure. To encourage the spirit to enter, the sculpture, wrapped in a red cloth, was placed on a gold plate and carried to the family house. There it received daily visits from the head of the household, who brought offerings of food and prayer.[1] This *iene*'s fine detailing, from the powerful head to the elegantly modeled limbs terminating in clearly articulated fingers, further attests to the importance of the spirit represented.

1. Riedel 1886, reprinted in New York, The Metropolitan Museum of Art, 1988b, p. 316, pl. 62.

49

Figure

Lesser Sunda Islands, Timor (probably
Tetum)[1]
19th–20th century
Wood
H. 62½ in. (158.8 cm)
Gift of Fred and Rita Richman, 1988
1988.143.164

Published: Hersey 1991, pl. 28

This wooden post represents a male figure with a concave face abstractly articulated by planes and volumes. The figure has an elongated torso, attenuated arms, and three rounded ridges in place of legs and feet; the topknot is similar to those on the funerary image from the Jörai of Vietnam (no. 58) and the figurated spoon from the Ifugao of the Philippines (no. 60).

Sacrificial posts such as this one played a significant role in rituals that honored ancestral spirits who presided over the land and instructed the Tetum in the raising of cattle, in agriculture, hunting and fishing, architecture, and social institutions. Not only did the ancestors pass on these traditions to the living; they also watched their descendants to ensure that customs were carefully followed, punishing those who failed to conform.[2] Offerings to the ancestral spirits were placed on stone slabs atop the sacrificial posts, which were sometimes adorned with textiles and jewelry.[3]

1. Tetum, also known as Belu, refers to the people and the language they speak; it is one of two major languages spoken on the island of Timor (Hicks 1988, p. 138).

2. Vroklage 1952, pp. 121–22.

3. New York, The Metropolitan Museum of Art, 1988b, p. 302.

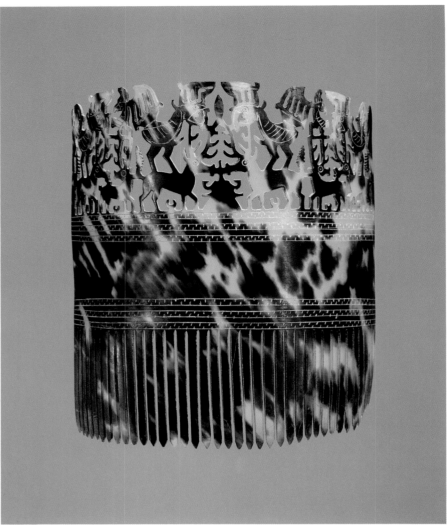

50

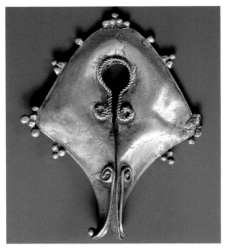

51

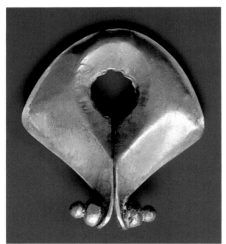

52

53, 54

50

Hai kara jangga

Lesser Sunda Islands, East Sumba
20th century
Tortoiseshell
H. 5¹/2 in. (14 cm)
Gift of Fred and Rita Richman, 1988
1988.143.125

Published: Richman 1980, fig. 6

51, 52

Two mamuli

Lesser Sunda Islands, East Sumba
19th–20th century
Metal alloy, gold
H. 3 in. (7.6 cm)
Gift of Fred and Rita Richman, 1988
51. 1988.143.145
52. 1988.143.146

53, 54

Pair of Bracelets

Lesser Sunda Islands, East Sumba
20th century
Ivory
Diam., each 3¹/2 in. (8.9 cm)
Gift of Fred and Rita Richman, 1988
53. 1988.143.126
54. 1988.143.127

Published: Richman 1980, fig. 10

On the island of Sumba, young women made known the fact that they had entered puberty by wearing intricately carved tortoiseshell combs. Such combs were also worn by adult noblewomen.[1] In this example (no. 50), bilaterally symmetrical groups of cocks perched on top of deer flank an abstracted central image, most likely representing the *andung*, or skull tree, where trophy heads were displayed. These animal and tree motifs replicate textile designs on *hinggi*, prestigious cloths worn by the Sumbanese male elite. The use of male-associated iconography on female headdresses is but one expression of the complementarity and opposition of the male and female in the art and culture of Sumba.

Another expression of male-female complementarity is evident in *mamuli*, omega-shaped ear ornaments (nos. 51, 52). While the earrings' distinctive outlines clearly allude to female reproductive powers, *mamuli* are classified as male goods in the ritual gift exchange that accompanies marriage.[2] Within the larger classification of *mamuli* as male goods, plain *mamuli* are considered a female type while those with long elaborate bases are considered a male type.[3]

In contrast to *mamuli*, ivory bracelets (nos. 53, 54) are classified as female goods, and they are presented by the bride's family to the groom's family. Other female goods, such as textiles, porcelain, beadwork, and, in former times, personal attendants, were given with the bracelets.[4] As reciprocal gifts, the groom's family would present the bride's family with metal objects, such as *mamuli*, brass bracelets, gold chains, and swords.

The ivory bangles are usually decorated, as these are, with incised circles arranged in a series of triangular configurations, a design that recalls the *tumpal* motif derived from Indian *patola* cloths traded widely throughout Southeast Asia. As in the ivory ornaments, the triangular *tumpal* motif was often employed on the borders of many types of Indonesian textiles.

1. Rodgers 1985, p. 329, no. 110.

2. Ibid., p. 330, no. 125.

3. See, for example, Taylor and Aragon 1991, p. 227.

4. Adams 1969, p. 47; Rodgers 1985, p. 332, no. 145.

55

Spinning Wheel

Lesser Sunda Islands, Sumba
19th–20th century
Wood, bamboo, fiber
H. 21 in. (53.3 cm)
Gift of Fred and Rita Richman, 1988
1988.143.169

Exhibited: New York, The Metropolitan Museum of Art, 1989

Published: Hersey 1991, pl. 26

In many Indonesian societies, weaving was closely associated with female powers of procreation. On the island of Sumba, the spinning of fibers into thread was seen as a metaphor for the fusing of the different components of the human soul into a new life inside the womb. Accordingly, young women were expected to master the art of spinning thread before marriage.[1]

Indonesian spinning wheels are generally composed of a spoked wheel rotated by a handle that turns a mounted spindle by means of a cord; only the bamboo wheel and wooden male figure supporting it remain in this example from Sumba.[2] Although the figure's arms are themselves not prominent and are carved in low relief on each side, the rotating spokes of the wheel cleverly create the illusion of an extraordinary being that is multilimbed. The use of this commanding male image to support a wheel used for the quintessentially female activity of spinning again conveys the complementarity of male and female in Sumbanese society.

1. Geirnaert 1989, p. 71, cited in Taylor and Aragon 1991, p. 227.

2. Hitchcock 1991, p. 32. Complete spinning wheels are illustrated in Taylor and Aragon 1991, p. 226, fig. 7.51; and Fraser-Lu 1989, p. 21, fig. 10.

56

Neck Ornament

Assam (Angami Naga)
19th–20th century
Shell, carnelian, glass beads, bone
L. 17 in. (43.2 cm)
Gift of Fred and Rita Richman, 1988
1988.143.92

Nearly eighteen hundred Naga tribes inhabit the mountainous Assam region on the northeastern border of India. Those most renowned for their ferocious resistance to Western colonization are the Angami, the "unconquered."[1] To mark his high status, an Angami warrior would wear this impressive necklace both in battle and during agricultural festivities, two important events symbolically associated with concepts of regeneration and fertility. In many Southeast Asian cultures, as among the Naga, the taking of enemy lives in battle as offerings to the gods was necessary to bring forth new life; hence warfare, the headhunt, and agriculture were all symbolically related. In addition to conceptual affinities, several aspects of material culture, such as the prominent use of buffalo horns, boars' tusks, and hornbill beaks as well as striped woven textiles and bead necklaces as signs of prestige, bring to mind parallels among other groups in Island Southeast Asia, notably the mountain peoples of Northern Luzon in the Philippines.

Angami necklaces can be distinguished from those of other Naga groups by their combination of specific types of beads and shell, among them lozenge-shaped conch, carnelian, blue glass, and yellow beads separated by bone spacers; whole or cut conch shells embellish the ends.[2] The beads are imported from the coasts and lowlands, their distant origins further enhancing the wearer's status.

1. The British, whose interests in the Assam region included the cultivation of tea leaves, began military expeditions against the Angami in 1835 (Rowney 1882, p. 168).

2. The conch-shell section is worn on the shoulders and back, the beaded section in front (Fürer-Haimendorf 1933, pl. opp. p. 17). Similar Angami necklaces are illustrated in Jacobs et al. 1990, pp. 328, 330, 332.

57

Neck Ornament

Assam (Naga)
19th–20th century
Copper alloy
Diam. 7 3/4 in. (19.7 cm)
Gift of Fred and Rita Richman, 1988
1988.143.115

Among the Naga, ornaments were worn not only for their beauty but as signifiers of individual and group identity. Imbued with power, the ornaments also had specific meanings and their use was restricted to different groups. Neck ornaments such as the one shown here were the prerogative of warriors.[1] A row of rounded projections in the form of human heads and spirals adorns the collar. The imagery of the human head signified success in the headhunt, an activity essential to agricultural productivity and the well-being of the community. When illness swept through the village, warriors would take a head to offer to the spirits. The taking of heads also ensured a good harvest, for human death was believed to generate agricultural fruition.

The headhunt generally involved three stages: ritual offerings would be made to the spirits; the headhunt would be carried out, after which the warriors would return to the village in a symbolically unclean state; and both warriors and trophy heads would then be ritually cleansed and reincorporated into society.[2] Among the Konyak Naga, clan elders would sprinkle rice beer over the heads while invoking the spirits of the dead, a ritual that had striking parallels among the mountain peoples of Taiwan, where the theme of fertility was similarly associated with the headhunt (see also no. 59).[3]

1. Fürer-Haimendorf 1933, pls. opposite pp. 179, 188; Barbier 1984, p. 38, fig. 6; Jacobs et al. 1990, pp. 103–14.

2. Jacobs et al. 1990, pp. 117–29.

3. Fürer-Haimendorf 1933, pp. 188–89.

58

Kut

Vietnam (Jörai)[1]
19th–20th century
Wood
H. 73 1/4 in. (186.1 cm)
Gift of Fred and Rita Richman, 1988
1988.143.81

Published: Hersey 1980, p. 73; Hersey
1991, p. 93

As noted earlier, the squatting human figure is a motif widespread in Island Southeast Asia; its meaning has been the subject of much speculation.[2] The most common interpretation is that it replicates both the burial and the fetal position, thus symbolizing death and rebirth. Another possible meaning is that, as a position frequently assumed by the living, its use in funerary figures alludes to the continuity of life after death.[3]

This carved Jörai funerary post, which portrays a squatting human figure in the knee-elbow-chin position, with elbows resting on knees and hands on chin, is said to represent a follower of the deceased who was sacrificed so that he could continue to serve his master in the afterlife.[4] It was formerly part of a rectangular funerary house, or *pösat*, each corner of which was guarded by a similar figurated post, or *kut*. Crossbeams inserted in the aperture below each *kut* restricted access to the tomb by forming a kind of fence around the funerary structure.[5] The carving of the posts was considered a sacred activity, and all other work by artists was forbidden while they were being made.[6]

The occurrence of the squatting figure in central Vietnam is intriguing, for the indigenous peoples, such as the Jörai, are among the earliest known inhabitants of a region that lies in the general direction of ancient migrations that populated the Indochinese peninsula and the Indonesian and Pacific islands.[7] One theory proposes that these groups, originating in the northwest, may have been the ancestors of those who came to be known as Indonesians.[8]

1. Called Moï by the Vietnamese, Phnong by the Khmer, Kha by the Lao, and Montagnards by the French, who first colonized them, the autochthonous peoples of central Vietnam make up several ethnic groups but have no common term by which they designate themselves (Dournes 1988, p. 27).

2. The so-called squatting figure was often depicted seated rather than actually squatting. Ch'en Ch'i-lu (1972) classifies the motif in Southeast Asia and the Pacific into four types: with arms raised in front of the chest (similar to the figure seen here and nos. 3–10, 45, and 60); with hands holding flexed legs (nos. 2, 17, 29); with arms folded and resting on the knees (nos. 47, 48); and an unconventional form. He suggests that the first two types are the earliest.

3. Although Hoog (1959, p. 96) does not discount the motif's possible association with the birth position, he dismisses the reference to death as far-fetched. It seems possible, however, that the image was intended to evoke a multiplicity of meanings.

4. Dournes 1968; Dournes 1988.

5. Illustrated, for example, in Baudesson [1919?], pl. opposite p. 100.

6. Dournes 1988, p. 28.

7. Coedès 1962, pp. 28–33; Dournes 1988, p. 27.

8. Dournes 1968, p. 92.

59

Panel

Taiwan (Paiwan)
19th–20th century
Wood
L. 31½ in. (80 cm)
Gift of Fred and Rita Richman, 1987
1987.453.4

Exhibited: New York, The Metropolitan
Museum of Art, 1988b, p. 340, pl. 74

The Paiwan inhabit the mountainous region of what is today southern Taiwan, thought to be a keystone in the cultural history of Island Southeast Asia.[1] Practices common to other Southeast Asian groups, such as the headhunt and the ceremonial distribution of wealth, and stylistic affinities in their art link the indigenous groups of Taiwan to their Indonesian[2] and Philippine neighbors. The cultural parallels strengthen the generally accepted notion that Austronesian migrants probably originating from the Asian mainland peopled the Southeast Asian and Pacific islands via Taiwan, Borneo, and the Philippines. It has been further suggested that Taiwan was the home of the proto-Austronesian language.

As in other cultures, distinctive architecture was an important mark of rank among the Paiwan. The nobleman's house was of special significance for it was considered the embodiment of the ancestors. This carved wooden panel once decorated an exterior wall of such a house.[3] A human head is carved in low relief at each end of the panel, and between them are two coiled snakes in reverse mirror image. Each face is outlined by a serrated band, while a double-headed snake adorns the forehead. The human head and snake motifs are believed to represent ancestors and probably allude to the headhunt as well. The snake motif is especially important, for the Paiwan believed that Vorun, the "hundred-pace snake," was the ancestor of the nobility. According to one version of the Paiwan origin myth, the sun descended to a mountaintop and laid two eggs, one red and the other white. Vorun sat on the eggs until they hatched, and from them emerged the first man and woman, the ancestors of the highest-ranking Paiwan families.[4] Representations of the snake were thus the prerogative of the aristocracy, while proper rules of behavior with respect to snakes were carefully observed by all.[5]

1. Bellwood 1979, p. 123.

2. Cameron 1985a, p. 161.

3. See, for example, the nobleman's house illustrated in McGovern 1923, p. 134 (reprinted in Cameron 1985a, p. 162, fig. 204), which shows similar panels beneath the roof eaves.

4. Ho 1967, vol. 2, pp. 249–50, cited in Cameron 1985a, p. 163.

5. Ch'en Ch'i-lu 1972, p. 401; Ch'en Ch'i-lu 1988, p. 188.

60

Spoon

Northern Luzon (Ifugao)
19th–20th century
Wood
H. 6³/₄ in. (17.2 cm)
Gift of Fred and Rita Richman, 1988
1988.143.137

The indigenous peoples inhabiting the mountains of the northern area of the island of Luzon in the Philippines, collectively known as the Igorots, from the Spanish word *igorrotes* ("mountain dwellers"), are generally divided into distinct cultural groups, among them the Ifugao, Kankanay, Tinguian, Kalinga, Bontoc, Ibaloi, Isneg, Gaddang, and Ilongot.[1] The most extensively studied of these groups are the Ifugao, renowned for their breathtaking rice terraces and for their figurative sculptures, among them rice guardian figures and figurated bowls and spoons, such as the one shown here.

The carved handle of this wooden spoon portrays a diminutive squatting figure with elbows resting on knees and hands on neck, a posture that echoes the monumental funerary image from Vietnam (no. 58) and smaller figures from Borneo (nos. 3–10) and Cenderawasih Bay (no. 45). It is known from Spanish colonial accounts that figurated wooden spoons and ladles have been used by the Ifugao for serving food and wine since the nineteenth century, perhaps even earlier. One Spanish missionary noted that "[the Ifugao] carved spoons sometimes with very objectionable figures in relief," probably alluding to handles depicting scenes of copulation.[2]

The earliest documented examples of figurated spoons are those exhibited in the encyclopedic "Exposición General de las Islas Filipinas," held in Madrid in 1887,[3] and a piece collected in the early 1880s by the French explorer Alfred Marche.[4] Their manufacture increased dramatically in the early twentieth century, when carvers began making them to sell commercially. It was not unusual for old spoons with plain handles to be recarved with human figures to satisfy the increased demand for the figurated version. The spoons continue to be used today. The carved image on the handle is referred to as *bin-nullol*, meaning something that resembles a guardian figure.[5]

1. Ellis 1981, pp. 184–85.

2. Villaverde 1909 (1879), cited in Ellis 1981, p. 215.

3. Madrid 1887. The objects in this exhibition form the core of the Philippine collection of the Museo Nacional de Etnología, Madrid. Examples of figurated spoons include acc. nos. IV-156, IV-161, IV-186, and IV-237.

4. Marche 1886, p. 208.

5. Conklin 1980, pp. 10, 35, figs. 50, 173; Peralta 1977, pp. 316–17.

Checklist of the Collection

BORNEO

Hampatong
Borneo, Kalimantan (Dayak)
19th–20th century
Wood
H. 71 in. (180.3 cm)
Gift of Fred and Rita Richman, 1988
1988.124.3
No. 1

Hampatong
Borneo, Kalimantan (Dayak)
19th–20th century
Wood
H. 44½ in. (113 cm)
Gift of Fred and Rita Richman, 1988
1988.143.1
No. 2

Figure
Borneo, Kalimantan (Dayak)
19th–20th century
Wood
H. 31½ in. (80 cm)
Gift of Fred and Rita Richman, 1988
1988.143.2

Hampatong

Borneo, Kalimantan (Dayak)
19th–20th century
Wood
H. 63 in. (160 cm)
Gift of Fred and Rita Richman, 1988
1988.143.5

Figure

Borneo, Kalimantan (Dayak)
19th–20th century
Wood
H. 29½ in. (74.9 cm)
Gift of Fred and Rita Richman, 1988
1988.143.51

Hook

Borneo, Kalimantan (Dayak)
19th–20th century
Wood
H. 27¾ in. (70.5 cm)
Gift of Fred and Rita Richman, 1988
1988.143.100

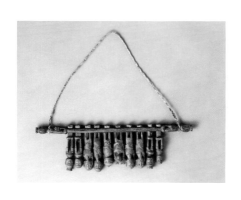

Sword

Borneo, Kalimantan (Dayak)
19th–20th century
Metal, bone
H. 29 in. (73.7 cm)
Gift of Fred and Rita Richman, 1988
1988.143.25

Charm

Borneo, Kalimantan (Dayak)
19th–20th century
Wood
L. 14¼ in. (36.2 cm)
Gift of Fred and Rita Richman, 1988
1988.143.94

Figure

Borneo, Kalimantan (Dayak)
19th–20th century
Wood
H. 6 in. (15.2 cm)
Gift of Fred and Rita Richman, 1988
1988.143.128

Figure

Borneo, Kalimantan (Dayak)
19th–20th century
Wood
H. 4½ in. (11.4 cm)
Gift of Fred and Rita Richman, 1988
1988.143.129

Figure

Borneo, Kalimantan (Dayak)
19th–20th century
Wood
H. 5 in. (12.7 cm)
Gift of Fred and Rita Richman, 1988
1988.143.132

Container

Borneo, Kalimantan (Dayak)
19th–20th century
Bamboo
H. 12 in. (30.5 cm)
Gift of Fred and Rita Richman, 1988
1988.143.151

Figure

Borneo, Kalimantan (Dayak)
19th–20th century
Wood
H. 4 in. (10.2 cm)
Gift of Fred and Rita Richman, 1988
1988.143.130

Figure

Borneo, Kalimantan (Dayak)
19th–20th century
Wood
H. 5 in. (12.7 cm)
Gift of Fred and Rita Richman, 1988
1988.143.144

Container

Borneo, Kalimantan (Dayak)
19th–20th century
Bamboo, wood
H. 5½ in. (14 cm)
Gift of Fred and Rita Richman, 1988
1988.143.152

Container

Borneo, Kalimantan (Dayak)
19th–20th century
Basketry
H. 13 in. (33 cm)
Gift of Fred and Rita Richman, 1988
1988.143.166

Hawat

Borneo (Kenyah or Kayan)
19th–20th century
Wood, shell, rattan
H. 12¼ in. (31.1 cm)
Gift of Fred and Rita Richman, 1987
1987.453.2
No. 13

Finial

Borneo, Kalimantan (Kenyah or Kayan)
19th–20th century
Wood
H. 39 in. (99.1 cm)
Gift of Fred and Rita Richman, 1988
1988.143.33

Hawat

Borneo, Kalimantan (Dayak)
19th–20th century
Basketry
H. 12½ in. (31.8 cm)
Gift of Fred and Rita Richman, 1988
1988.143.167

Shield

Borneo, Kalimantan or Sarawak (Kenyah or Kayan)
19th–20th century
Wood, pigment, human hair, rattan
H. 56 in. (142.2 cm)
Gift of Fred and Rita Richman, 1988
1988.143.19

Hawat

Borneo (Kenyah or Kayan)
20th century
Beads, rattan, wood, fabric, shell, teeth
H. 13 in. (33 cm)
Gift of Fred and Rita Richman, 1988
1988.143.52
No. 12

Hudoq

Borneo, Kalimantan or Sarawak (Kenyah or Kayan)
19th–20th century
Wood, rattan, fabric, feather, glass
H. 17½ in. (44.5 cm)
Gift of Fred and Rita Richman, 1988
1988.143.55

Figure

Borneo, Kalimantan (Kenyah or Kayan)
19th–20th century
Wood
H. 16¼ in. (41.3 cm)
Gift of Fred and Rita Richman, 1988
1988.143.61

Hudoq

Borneo, Kalimantan (Kenyah or Kayan)
19th–20th century
Wood, pigment, rattan
H. 17 in. (43.2 cm)
Gift of Fred and Rita Richman, 1988
1988.143.77
No. 11

Mask

Borneo, Kalimantan (Kenyah or Kayan)
19th–20th century
Wood
H. 7 in. (17.8 cm)
Gift of Fred and Rita Richman, 1988
1988.143.60

Kiang

Borneo, Kalimantan or Sarawak (Kenyah or Kayan)
19th–20th century
Wood, mother-of-pearl
H. 24¾ in. (62.9 cm)
Gift of Fred and Rita Richman, 1988
1988.143.71

Hudoq

Borneo, Kalimantan or Sarawak (Kenyah or Kayan)
19th–20th century
Wood, paint, hair
H. 14½ in. (36.8 cm)
Gift of Fred and Rita Richman, 1988
1988.143.78

Figure

Borneo, Kalimantan (Kenyah or Kayan)
19th–20th century
Wood
H. 33¹/₂ in. (85.1 cm)
Gift of Fred and Rita Richman, 1988
1988.143.99

Container

Borneo, Kalimantan (Kenyah or Kayan)
19th–20th century
Beads, fabric, basketry
H. 8 in. (20.3 cm)
Gift of Fred and Rita Richman, 1988
1988.143.134

Tuntun

Borneo, Sarawak (Iban)
19th–20th century
Wood
H. 21¹/₄ in. (54 cm)
Gift of Fred and Rita Richman, 1988
1988.143.10

Sabau Ear Ornament

Borneo, Kalimantan (Kenyah)
19th–20th century
Hornbill beak
H. 5¹/₂ in. (14 cm)
Gift of Fred and Rita Richman, 1988
1988.143.131

Hudoq

Borneo, Kalimantan or Sarawak (Kenyah or Kayan)
19th–20th century
Wood, pigment, rattan
H. 15⁵/₈ in. (39.7 cm)
Gift of Fred and Rita Richman, 1988
1988.143.156

Tuntun

Borneo, Sarawak (Iban)
19th–20th century
Wood
H. 21¹/₄ in. (54 cm)
Gift of Fred and Rita Richman, 1988
1988.143.11
No. 4

Tuntun

Borneo, Sarawak (Iban)
19th–20th century
Wood
H. 20 in. (50.8 cm)
Gift of Fred and Rita Richman, 1988
1988.143.12
No. 5

Tuntun

Borneo, Sarawak (Iban)
19th–20th century
Wood
H. 20½ in. (52.1 cm)
Gift of Fred and Rita Richman, 1988
1988.143.14
No. 7

Tuntun

Borneo, Sarawak (Iban)
19th–20th century
Wood
H. 21 in. (53.3 cm)
Gift of Fred and Rita Richman, 1988
1988.143.16
No. 9

Tuntun

Borneo, Sarawak (Iban)
19th–20th century
Wood
H. 21 in. (53.3 cm)
Gift of Fred and Rita Richman, 1988
1988.143.13
No. 6

Tuntun

Borneo, Sarawak (Iban)
19th–20th century
Wood
H. 22¾ in. (57.8 cm)
Gift of Fred and Rita Richman, 1988
1988.143.15
No. 8

Tuntun

Borneo, Sarawak (Iban)
19th–20th century
Wood
H. 21½ in. (54.6 cm)
Gift of Fred and Rita Richman, 1988
1988.143.18
No. 10

Tuntun

Borneo, Sarawak (Iban)
19th–20th century
Wood
H. 21 in. (53.3 cm)
Gift of Fred and Rita Richman, 1988
1988.143.17
No. 3

Naga morsarang

North Sumatra (Batak)
19th–20th century
Water buffalo horn, wood
L. 20½ in. (52.1 cm)
Gift of Fred and Rita Richman, 1987
1987.453.1
No. 19

Tunggal panaluan

North Sumatra (Batak)
19th–20th century
Wood, fiber, hair
H. 71 in. (180.3 cm)
Gift of Fred and Rita Richman, 1988
1988.124.1
No. 16

Figure

Borneo, Sarawak (Melanu)
19th–20th century
Bone
H. 3½ in. (8.9 cm)
Gift of Fred and Rita Richman, 1988
1988.143.159

Si gale-gale

North Sumatra (Batak)
19th–20th century
Wood, metal
H. 11¼ in. (28.6 cm)
Gift of Fred and Rita Richman, 1987
1987.453.6
No. 27

Pupuk Container

North Sumatra (Batak)
19th–20th century
Ceramic, wood
H. 13½ in. (34.4 cm)
Gift of Fred and Rita Richman, 1988
1988.124.2a,b
No. 20

Door

North Sumatra (Batak)

19th–20th century

Wood

H. 38 in. (96.5 cm)

Gift of Fred and Rita Richman, 1988

1988.143.3

Architectural Panel

Sumatra (Batak)

19th–20th century

Wood

L. 48 in. (121.9 cm)

Gift of Fred and Rita Richman, 1988

1988.143.9

Door

North Sumatra (Batak)

19th–20th century

Wood

H. 40 in. (101.6 cm)

Gift of Fred and Rita Richman, 1988

1988.143.21

Gana-gana

North Sumatra (Batak)

19th–20th century

Wood, fiber, fabric, shell, metal

H. 41 in. (104.1 cm)

Gift of Fred and Rita Richman, 1988

1988.143.6

No. 26

Singa

North Sumatra (Batak)

19th–20th century

Wood, pigment

H. 39 in. (99.1 cm)

Gift of Fred and Rita Richman, 1988

1988.143.20

Knife

North Sumatra (Batak)

19th–20th century

Metal, buffalo horn

H. 21 in. (53.3 cm)

Gift of Fred and Rita Richman, 1988

1988.143.23

Piso sanalenggam

North Sumatra (Batak)
19th–20th century
Metal, water buffalo horn
H. 21 in. (53.3 cm)
Gift of Fred and Rita Richman, 1988
1988.143.24
No. 31

Singa

North Sumatra (Batak)
19th–20th century
Wood
H. 55 in. (139.7 cm)
Gift of Fred and Rita Richman, 1988
1988.143.28
No. 15

Singa

North Sumatra (Batak)
19th–20th century
Wood
H. 50 in. (127 cm)
Gift of Fred and Rita Richman, 1988
1988.143.30

Singa

North Sumatra (Batak)
19th–20th century
Wood
H. 55 in. (139.7 cm)
Gift of Fred and Rita Richman, 1988
1988.143.27
No. 14

Singa

North Sumatra (Batak)
19th–20th century
Wood
H. 43 in. (109.2 cm)
Gift of Fred and Rita Richman, 1988
1988.143.29

Pupuk Container

North Sumatra (Batak)
Late 19th–early 20th century
Ceramic, wood
H. 12 in. (30.5 cm)
Gift of Fred and Rita Richman, 1988
1988.143.37
No. 24

Pupuk Container

North Sumatra (Batak)
19th–early 20th century
Ceramic, wood
H. 10 in. (25.4 cm)
Gift of Fred and Rita Richman, 1988
1988.143.38
No. 23

Pupuk Container

North Sumatra (Batak)
19th–early 20th century
Ceramic, wood
H. 6½ in. (16.5 cm)
Gift of Fred and Rita Richman, 1988
1988.143.40
No. 22

Figure

North Sumatra (Batak)
19th–20th century
Wood, fiber, hair
H. 17½ in. (44.5 cm)
Gift of Fred and Rita Richman, 1988
1988.143.42

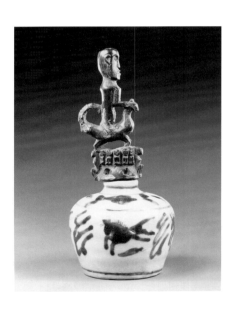

Pupuk Container

North Sumatra (Batak)
19th–early 20th century
Ceramic, wood
H. 7½ in. (19.1 cm)
Gift of Fred and Rita Richman, 1988
1988.143.39
No. 21

Pupuk Container

North Sumatra (Batak)
19th–20th century
Ceramic, wood
H. 4½ in. (11.4 cm)
Gift of Fred and Rita Richman, 1988
1988.143.41

Si gale-gale

North Sumatra (Batak)
19th–20th century
Wood, fabric, metal
H. 21½ in. (54.6 cm)
Gift of Fred and Rita Richman, 1988
1988.143.47
No. 28

Figure

North Sumatra (Batak)
19th–20th century
Wood
H. 27 in. (68.6 cm)
Gift of Fred and Rita Richman, 1988
1988.143.48

Musical Instrument

North Sumatra (Batak)
19th–20th century
Wood
H. 28 in. (71.1 cm)
Gift of Fred and Rita Richman, 1988
1988.143.50
No. 30

Figure

North Sumatra (Batak)
19th–20th century
Wood
H. 17¼ in. (43.8 cm)
Gift of Fred and Rita Richman, 1988
1988.143.57

Figure

North Sumatra (Batak)
19th–20th century
Wood
H. 17¼ in. (43.8 cm)
Gift of Fred and Rita Richman, 1988
1988.143.58

Figure

North Sumatra (Batak)
19th–20th century
Stone
H. 12 in. (30.5 cm)
Gift of Fred and Rita Richman, 1988
1988.143.49

Singa

North Sumatra (Batak)
19th–20th century
Wood
H. 21 in. (53.3 cm)
Gift of Fred and Rita Richman, 1988
1988.143.56

Horse Head

North Sumatra (Batak)
19th–20th century
Wood
L. 13½ in. (34.3 cm)
Gift of Fred and Rita Richman, 1988
1988.143.68

Manuk-manuk

North Sumatra (Batak)
19th–20th century
Wood
H. 14 in. (35.6 cm)
Gift of Fred and Rita Richman, 1988
1988.143.75

Figure

North Sumatra (Batak)
19th–20th century
Stone
H. 27½ in. (69.9 cm)
Gift of Fred and Rita Richman, 1988
1988.143.79

Singa

North Sumatra (Batak)
19th–20th century
Wood
H. 49 in. (124.5 cm)
Gift of Fred and Rita Richman, 1988
1988.143.70

Architectural Panel

North Sumatra (Batak)
19th–20th century
Wood
H. 37 in. (94 cm)
Gift of Fred and Rita Richman, 1988
1988.143.76

Figure

North Sumatra (Batak)
19th–20th century
Stone
H. 25½ in. (64.8 cm)
Gift of Fred and Rita Richman, 1988
1988.143.80

Hombung Chest

North Sumatra (Batak)
19th–20th century
Wood
H. 77½ in. (196.9 cm)
Gift of Fred and Rita Richman, 1988
1988.143.83

Tunggal panaluan

North Sumatra (Batak)
19th–20th century
Wood, fiber, hair
H. 68 in. (172.7 cm)
Gift of Fred and Rita Richman, 1988
1988.143.85

Tunggal panaluan

North Sumatra (Batak)
19th–20th century
Wood
H. 64 in. (162.6 cm)
Gift of Fred and Rita Richman, 1988
1988.143.87

Tunggal panaluan

North Sumatra (Batak)
19th–20th century
Wood, fabric, hair
H. 70 in. (177.8 cm)
Gift of Fred and Rita Richman, 1988
1988.143.84

Tunggal panaluan

North Sumatra (Batak)
19th–20th century
Wood, hair, fiber
H. 60 in. (152.4 cm)
Gift of Fred and Rita Richman, 1988
1988.143.86

Tunggal panaluan

North Sumatra (Batak)
19th–20th century
Wood, fabric, hair
H. 67 in. (170.2 cm)
Gift of Fred and Rita Richman, 1988
1988.143.88

Tunggal panaluan

North Sumatra (Batak)

19th–20th century

Wood, fabric, hair

H. 66 in. (167.6 cm)

Gift of Fred and Rita Richman, 1988

1988.143.89

Figure

North Sumatra (Batak)

19th–20th century

Stone

H. 33 in. (83.8 cm)

Gift of Fred and Rita Richman, 1988

1988.143.95

Handle

North Sumatra (Batak)

19th–20th century

Buffalo horn

H. 7 in. (17.8 cm)

Gift of Fred and Rita Richman, 1988

1988.143.112

Tungkot malehat

North Sumatra (Batak)

19th–20th century

Wood, fiber, feathers

H. 58¹/₂ in. (148.6 cm)

Gift of Fred and Rita Richman, 1988

1988.143.90

No. 17

Figure

North Sumatra (Batak)

19th–20th century

Wood

H. 7 in. (17.8 cm)

Gift of Fred and Rita Richman, 1988

1988.143.111

No. 29

Figure

North Sumatra (Batak)

19th–20th century

Wood

H. 6³/₄ in. (17.2 cm)

Gift of Fred and Rita Richman, 1988

1988.143.113

No. 33

Ear Ornament

North Sumatra (Batak)
19th–20th century
Brass
H. 6¼ in. (15.9 cm)
Gift of Fred and Rita Richman, 1988
1988.143.114

Shot Holder

North Sumatra (Batak)
19th–20th century
Buffalo horn, lead
H. 6½ in. (16.5 cm)
Gift of Fred and Rita Richman, 1988
1988.143.138a, b

Knife

North Sumatra (Batak)
19th–20th century
Metal, wood
H. 10¾ in. (27.3 cm)
Gift of Fred and Rita Richman, 1988
1988.143.140

Pustaha

North Sumatra (Batak)
19th–20th century
Wood, bark, pigment
H. 7¾ in. (19.7 cm)
Gift of Fred and Rita Richman, 1988
1988.143.133
No. 25

Parpanggalahan

North Sumatra (Batak)
19th–20th century
Water buffalo horn, wood
H. 7¼ in. (18.4 cm)
Gift of Fred and Rita Richman, 1988
1988.143.139
No. 32

Figure

North Sumatra (Batak)
19th–20th century
Copper alloy
H. 4½ in. (11.4 cm)
Gift of Fred and Rita Richman, 1988
1988.143.141
No. 18

Bracelet
North Sumatra (Batak)
19th–20th century
Brass
D. 3¼ in. (8.3 cm)
Gift of Fred and Rita Richman, 1988
1988.143.142

Container
North Sumatra (Batak)
19th–20th century
Ivory
H. 2¼ in. (5.7 cm)
Gift of Fred and Rita Richman, 1988
1988.143.149

Mask
North Sumatra (Batak)
19th–20th century
Wood
H. 12½ in. (31.8 cm)
Gift of Fred and Rita Richman, 1988
1988.143.154

Figure
North Sumatra (Batak)
19th–20th century
Metal alloy
H. 4 in. (10.2 cm)
Gift of Fred and Rita Richman, 1988
1988.143.143

Container
North Sumatra (Batak)
19th–20th century
Bamboo, wood
H. 5 in. (12.7 cm)
Gift of Fred and Rita Richman, 1988
1988.143.150

Mask
North Sumatra (Batak)
19th–20th century
Wood
H. 9¼ in. (23.5 cm)
Gift of Fred and Rita Richman, 1988
1988.143.155

Mask
North Sumatra (Batak)
19th–20th century
Wood
H. 9 in. (22.9 cm)
Gift of Fred and Rita Richman, 1988
1988.143.157

Figure
North Sumatra (Batak)
19th–20th century
Wood
H. 5³/₄ in. (14.6 cm)
Gift of Fred and Rita Richman, 1988
1988.143.161

Singa
North Sumatra (Batak)
19th–20th century
Wood
H. 27 in. (68.6 cm)
Gift of Fred and Rita Richman, 1988
1988.143.170

Bone
North Sumatra (Batak)
19th–20th century
Bone
H. 4 in. (10.2 cm)
Gift of Fred and Rita Richman, 1988
1988.143.158

Pair of Figures
North Sumatra (Batak)
19th–20th century
Wood
H. 9 in. (22.9 cm); H. 9¹/₄ in. (23.5 cm)
Gift of Fred and Rita Richman, 1988
1988.143.163a, b

Headdress
West Sumatra (Minangkabau)
19th–20th century
Wood, gold leaf
L. 10¹/₄ in. (26 cm)
Gift of Fred and Rita Richman, 1988
1988.143.120
No. 34

Gelang gadang polang

West Sumatra (Minangkabau)
19th–20th century
Wood, metal, gold leaf
Diam. 5³/₄ in. (14.6 cm)
Gift of Fred and Rita Richman, 1988
1988.143.121
No. 35

Besihung

Lampung
19th–20th century
Iron
L. 18¹/₂ in. (47 cm)
Gift of Fred and Rita Richman, 1988
1988.143.171

Siraha salawa

Nias
19th–20th century
Wood
H. 25 in. (63.5 cm)
Gift of Fred and Rita Richman, 1987
1987.453.3
No. 37

Kris

West Sumatra (Minangkabau)
19th–20th century
Metal, bone
H. 19³/₄ in. (50.2 cm)
Gift of Fred and Rita Richman, 1988
1988.143.123

Besihung

Lampung
19th–20th century
Iron
L. 18¹/₂ in. (47 cm)
Gift of Fred and Rita Richman, 1988
1988.143.172
No. 36

Figure

Nias
19th–20th century
Stone
H. 37 in. (94 cm)
Gift of Fred and Rita Richman, 1988
1988.143.4

Sword

Nias
19th–20th century
Metal
H. 27½ in. (69.9 cm)
Gift of Fred and Rita Richman, 1988
1988.143.26

Hazi nuwu

Nias (probably Batu Islands)
19th–20th century
Wood, bamboo, rattan
H. 13½ in. (34.3 cm)
Gift of Fred and Rita Richman, 1988
1988.143.63
No. 40

Adu zatua

Nias
19th–20th century
Wood
H. 14¾ in. (37.5 cm)
Gift of Fred and Rita Richman, 1988
1988.143.65
No. 39

Adu zatua

Nias
19th–20th century
Wood
H. 12 in. (30.5 cm)
Gift of Fred and Rita Richman, 1988
1988.143.62

Adu zatua

Nias
19th–20th century
Wood
H. 14 in. (35.6 cm)
Gift of Fred and Rita Richman, 1988
1988.143.64
No. 38

Adu zatua

Nias
19th–20th century
Wood
H. 14½ in. (36.8 cm)
Gift of Fred and Rita Richman, 1988
1988.143.66

Figure

Nias
19th–20th century
Wood
H. 19¼ in. (48.9 cm)
Gift of Fred and Rita Richman, 1988
1988.143.67

Kareau

Nicobar Islands
19th–20th century
Wood
H. 32 in. (81.3 cm)
Gift of Fred and Rita Richman, 1988
1988.143.96
No. 41

Kris

Java
19th–20th century
Ivory, metal
H. 26 in. (66 cm)
Gift of Fred and Rita Richman, 1988
1988.143.22

Neck Ornament

Nias
19th–20th century
Coconut shell
D. 8½ in. (21.6 cm)
Gift of Fred and Rita Richman, 1988
1988.143.118

Dog

Nicobar Islands
19th–20th century
Wood
L. 32½ in. (82.6 cm)
Gift of Fred and Rita Richman, 1988
1988.143.97

Blade

East Java or Bali, Dongson style
3rd century (?)
Bronze
H. 3 in. (7.6 cm)
Gift of Fred and Rita Richman, 1988
1988.143.108

SULAWESI

Blade

East Java or Bali, Dongson style
3rd century (?)
Bronze
H. 6½ in. (16.5 cm)
Gift of Fred and Rita Richman, 1988
1988.143.109

Implements on Chain

Java
19th–20th century
Silver
L. 25½ in. (64.8 cm)
Gift of Fred and Rita Richman, 1988
1988.143.122

Tau-tau

South Sulawesi (Sa'dan Toraja)
19th–20th century
Wood
H. 47½ in. (120.7 cm)
Gift of Fred and Rita Richman, 1988
1988.143.91
No. 42

Blade

East Java or Bali, Dongson style
3rd century (?)
Bronze
H. 10 in. (25.4 cm)
Gift of Fred and Rita Richman, 1988
1988.143.110

Handle

Java or Madura
19th–20th century
Ivory
H. 4¾ in. (12.1 cm)
Gift of Fred and Rita Richman, 1988
1988.143.160

Sanggori

Central Sulawesi
19th–20th century
Metal alloy
H. 8 in. (20.3 cm)
Gift of Fred and Rita Richman, 1988
1988.143.117
No. 43

Spoon

Sulawesi
19th–20th century
Wood
H. 5 in. (12.7 cm)
Gift of Fred and Rita Richman, 1988
1988.143.136

Pair of Earrings

Sulawesi
19th–20th century
Metal
H. 2 in. (5.1 cm)
Gift of Fred and Rita Richman, 1988
1988.143.148a, b

Korwar

Irian Jaya, Cenderawasih Bay
19th–20th century
Wood, beads, pigment
H. 11 in. (27.9 cm)
Gift of Fred and Rita Richman, 1988
1988.143.45
No. 45

IRIAN JAYA

Pair of Earrings

Sulawesi
19th–20th century
Metal
H. 4 in. (10.2 cm)
Gift of Fred and Rita Richman, 1988
1988.143.147a, b

Panel

Irian Jaya, Cenderawasih Bay
19th–20th century
Wood
H. 44½ in. (113 cm)
Gift of Fred and Rita Richman, 1988
1988.143.35

Figure

Irian Jaya, Cenderawasih Bay
19th–20th century
Wood
H. 8 in. (20.3 cm)
Gift of Fred and Rita Richman, 1988
1988.143.46

Neckrest

Irian Jaya, Cenderawasih Bay
19th–20th century
Wood
L. 10½ in. (26.7 cm)
Gift of Fred and Rita Richman, 1988
1988.143.59

Canoe Prow

Irian Jaya, Cenderawasih Bay
19th–20th century
Wood
H. 34 in. (86.4 cm)
Gift of Fred and Rita Richman, 1988
1988.143.74

Lime Container

Irian Jaya, Cenderawasih Bay
19th–20th century
Bamboo
H. 5¾ in. (14.6 cm)
Gift of Fred and Rita Richman, 1988
1988.143.153

RAJAH AMPAT ISLANDS

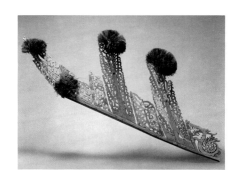

Canoe Prow

Irian Jaya, Cenderawasih Bay
19th–20th century
Wood
H. 37 in. (94 cm)
Gift of Fred and Rita Richman, 1988
1988.143.73

Canoe Prow

Irian Jaya, Cenderawasih Bay
19th–20th century
Wood, cassowary feathers, pigment
L. 58 in. (147.3 cm)
Gift of Fred and Rita Richman, 1988
1988.143.82
No. 44

Rooster

Rajah Ampat Islands
19th–20th century
Wood
H. 26½ in. (67.3 cm)
Gift of Fred and Rita Richman, 1988
1988.143.69 a, b

Iene

Southeast Moluccas, Leti style
19th–20th century
Wood
H. 13³/₄ in. (34.9 cm)
Gift of Fred and Rita Richman, 1987
1987.453.5
No. 48

Iene

Southeast Moluccas, Leti style
19th–20th century
Wood
H. 6 in. (15.2 cm)
Gift of Fred and Rita Richman, 1988
1988.143.54

Iene

Southeast Moluccas, Leti style
19th–20th century
Wood
H. 16¹/₂ in. (41.9 cm)
Gift of Fred and Rita Richman, 1988
1988.143.103

Iene

Southeast Moluccas, Leti style
19th–20th century
Wood
H. 5¹/₄ in. (13.3 cm)
Gift of Fred and Rita Richman, 1988
1988.143.53

Iene

Southeast Moluccas, probably Kai Islands,
Leti style
19th century
Wood
H. 22³/₄ in. (57.8 cm)
Gift of Fred and Rita Richman, 1988
1988.143.102
No. 47

Iene

Southeast Moluccas, Leti style
19th–20th century
Wood
H. 13 in. (33 cm)
Gift of Fred and Rita Richman, 1988
1988.143.104

Iene

Southeast Moluccas, Leti style
19th–20th century
Wood
H. 9 in. (22.9 cm)
Gift of Fred and Rita Richman, 1988
1988.143.105
No. 46

Spatula

Southeast Moluccas, Leti style
19th–20th century
Wood
H. 9³/₄ in. (24.8 cm)
Gift of Fred and Rita Richman, 1988
1988.143.107

Staff

Southeast Moluccas
19th–20th century
Wood
H. 43 in. (109.2 cm)
Gift of Fred and Rita Richman, 1988
1988.143.36

Figure

Southeast Moluccas, Leti style
19th–20th century
Wood
H. 6¹/₂ in. (16.5 cm)
Gift of Fred and Rita Richman, 1988
1988.143.106

Figure

Southeast Moluccas, Leti style
19th–20th century
Wood
H. 21 in. (53.3 cm)
Gift of Fred and Rita Richman, 1988
1988.143.119

Shield

North Moluccas, probably Halmahera
19th–20th century
Wood
H. 20 in. (50.8 cm)
Gift of Fred and Rita Richman, 1988
1988.143.32

Three Figures

Lesser Sunda Islands, Atauro
19th–20th century
Wood
H. 13¼ in. (33.7 cm)
Gift of Fred and Rita Richman, 1988
1988.143.43

Figure

Lesser Sunda Islands, Timor
19th–20th century
Wood
H. 54 in. (137.2 cm)
Gift of Fred and Rita Richman, 1988
1988.143.98

Figure

Lesser Sunda Islands, Timor (probably
Tetum)
19th–20th century
Wood
H. 62½ in. (158.8 cm)
Gift of Fred and Rita Richman, 1988
1988.143.164
No. 49

Figure

Lesser Sunda Islands, Atauro
19th–20th century
Wood
H. 8 in. (20.3 cm)
Gift of Fred and Rita Richman, 1988
1988.143.44

Figure

Lesser Sunda Islands, Timor
19th–20th century
Stone
H. 30½ in. (77.5 cm)
Gift of Fred and Rita Richman, 1988
1988.143.101

Figure

Lesser Sunda Islands, Timor
19th–20th century
Wood
H. 36 in. (91.4 cm)
Gift of Fred and Rita Richman, 1988
1988.143.165

Hai kara jangga

Lesser Sunda Islands, Sumba
20th century
Tortoiseshell
H. 5¹/₂ in. (14 cm)
Gift of Fred and Rita Richman, 1988
1988.143.124

Bracelet

Lesser Sunda Islands, East Sumba
20th century
Ivory
Diam. 3¹/₂ in. (8.9 cm)
Gift of Fred and Rita Richman, 1988
1988.143.126
No. 53

Bracelet

Lesser Sunda Islands, East Sumba
20th century
Ivory
Diam. 3¹/₂ in. (8.9 cm)
Gift of Fred and Rita Richman, 1988
1988.143.127
No. 54

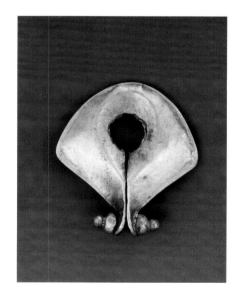

Hai kara jangga

Lesser Sunda Islands, East Sumba
20th century
Tortoiseshell
H. 5¹/₂ in. (14 cm)
Gift of Fred and Rita Richman, 1988
1988.143.125
No. 50

Mamuli

Lesser Sunda Islands, East Sumba
19th–20th century
Metal alloy, gold
H. 3 in. (7.6 cm)
Gift of Fred and Rita Richman, 1988
1988.143.145
No. 51

Mamuli

Lesser Sunda Islands, East Sumba
19th–20th century
Metal alloy, gold
H. 3 in. (7.6 cm)
Gift of Fred and Rita Richman, 1988
1988.143.146
No. 52

Pair of House Posts

Lesser Sunda Islands, Sumba
19th–20th century
Wood
H. 70 in. (177.8 cm)
Gift of Fred and Rita Richman, 1988
1988.143.168a, b

Handle

Lesser Sunda Islands, Lombok
19th–20th century
Buffalo horn
H. 4¼ in. (10.8 cm)
Gift of Fred and Rita Richman, 1988
1988.143.135

Neck Ornament

Assam (Naga)
19th–20th century
Beads, shell
L. 15½ in. (39.4 cm)
Gift of Fred and Rita Richman, 1988
1988.143.93

ASSAM

Spinning Wheel

Lesser Sunda Islands, Sumba
19th–20th century
Wood, bamboo, fiber
H. 21 in. (53.3 cm)
Gift of Fred and Rita Richman, 1988
1988.143.169
No. 55

Neck Ornament

Assam (Angami Naga)
19th–20th century
Shell, carnelian, glass beads, bone
L. 17 in. (43.2 cm)
Gift of Fred and Rita Richman, 1988
1988.143.92
No. 56

Neck Ornament

Assam (Naga)
19th–20th century
Copper alloy
Diam. 7¾ in. (19.7 cm)
Gift of Fred and Rita Richman, 1988
1988.143.115
No. 57

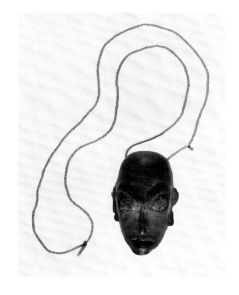

Neck Ornament

Assam (Naga)
19th–20th century
Brass
Diam. 6¹/₂ in. (16.5 cm)
Gift of Fred and Rita Richman, 1988
1988.143.116

Arm Ornament

Assam (Naga)
19th–20th century
Metal
H. 4 in. (10.2 cm)
Gift of Fred and Rita Richman, 1988
1988.143.174

Neck Ornament

Assam (Naga)
19th–20th century
Wood
H. 3¹/₂ in. (8.9 cm)
Gift of Fred and Rita Richman, 1988
1988.143.176

VIETNAM

Neck Ornament

Assam (Naga)
19th–20th century
Brass, beads
L. 5 in. (12.7 cm)
Gift of Fred and Rita Richman, 1988
1988.143.173

Neck Ornament

Assam (Naga)
19th–20th century
Brass, beads
H. 6¹/₂ in. (16.5 cm)
Gift of Fred and Rita Richman, 1988
1988.143.175

Kut

Vietnam (Jörai)
19th–20th century
Wood
H. 73¹/₄ in. (186.1 cm)
Gift of Fred and Rita Richman, 1988
1988.143.81
No. 58

Panel

Taiwan (Paiwan)
19th–20th century
Wood
L. 31½ in. (80 cm)
Gift of Fred and Rita Richman, 1987
1987.453.4
No. 59

Plate

Taiwan (Paiwan)
19th–20th century
Wood
Diam. 16 in. (40.6 cm)
Gift of Fred and Rita Richman, 1988
1988.143.8

Panel

Taiwan (Paiwan)
19th–20th century
Wood
H. 15 in. (38.1 cm)
Gift of Fred and Rita Richman, 1988
1988.143.72

Figure

Taiwan (Paiwan)
19th–20th century
Wood
H. 51 in. (129.5 cm)
Gift of Fred and Rita Richman, 1988
1988.143.7

Panel

Taiwan (Paiwan)
19th–20th century
Wood
H. 56 in. (142.2 cm)
Gift of Fred and Rita Richman, 1988
1988.143.34

Snake

Taiwan (Paiwan)
19th–20th century
Wood
H. 3¾ in. (9.5 cm)
Gift of Fred and Rita Richman, 1988
1988.143.177

Comb

Taiwan (Paiwan)
19th–20th century
Wood
H. 3³/₄ in. (9.5 cm)
Gift of Fred and Rita Richman, 1988
1988.143.178

Spoon

Northern Luzon (Ifugao)
19th–20th century
Wood
H. 6³/₄ in. (17.2 cm)
Gift of Fred and Rita Richman, 1988
1988.143.137
No. 60

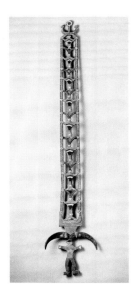

Post

Taiwan (Yami)
19th–20th century
Wood
H. 91 in. (231.1 cm)
Gift of Fred and Rita Richman, 1988
1988.143.162

Container

Northern Luzon
19th–20th century
Basketry
H. 12 in. (30.5 cm)
Gift of Fred and Rita Richman, 1988
1988.143.31

Glossary

adu zatua (Nias) Carved figure of a deceased person.

aso (Borneo) Dog motif used in textiles and sculpture.

begu (North Sumatra) Spirit released upon a person's death; distinct from a *tondi*.

besihung (Lampung) Forged iron container for soot used in the ritual blackening of teeth.

datu (North Sumatra) Ritual specialist.

gana-gana (North Sumatra) Carved anthropomorphic image.

gelang gadang polang (West Sumatra) Bracelet worn by young girls.

guru (North Sumatra) Master ritual specialist.

hai kara jangga (Sumba) Carved tortoise-shell comb worn by young women.

hampatong (Borneo) Protective figure depicting a spirit or a high-ranking ancestor.

hawat (Borneo) Baby carrier.

hazi nuwu (Nias, Batu Islands) Carved figure representing a deceased person.

hudoq (Borneo) Mask worn during agricultural rituals.

iene (Leti) Figure carved shortly after a person's death to serve as a receptacle for the departed spirit.

iwi (Nicobar Islands) Spirits causing sickness or death.

kareau (Nicobar Islands) Carved protective figure.

kendi A spouted ceramic container.

korwar (Cenderawasih Bay) Figure carved after a person's death to serve as a receptacle for the departed spirit.

kuku (West Sumatra) Fingernail motif used in woodcarving.

kut (Vietnam) Figurated wooden post guarding each of the four corners of a Jörai funerary house.

mamuli (Sumba) Omega-shaped ornament of gold or silver.

manuk-manuk In Batak mythology, a magical chicken that laid three eggs from which emerged the three principal deities, Batara Guru, Soripada, and Mangalabulan; also refers to carved images of a chicken.

martaban Large ceramic jar manufactured for export in Chinese and Southeast Asian kilns.

naga Powerful serpent-dragon in the mythology of many Southeast Asian cultures.

naga morsarang (North Sumatra) Ritual container made of water buffalo horn.

pangulubalang (North Sumatra) Captive spirit of a ritually executed human being; also refers to carved figures animated by the *pangulubalang*.

parpanggalahan (North Sumatra) Gunpowder container made of water buffalo horn.

pio-pio-tangguhan (North Sumatra) Sacred tree from which the *tunggal panaluan* staff is carved.

piso sanalenggam (North Sumatra) Single-edged sword with a carved handle made of water buffalo horn.

pucuak rabuang (West Sumatra) Bamboo shoot motif used in woodcarving and weaving.

pupuk (North Sumatra) A powerful mixture of organic substances prepared by a *datu*.

pustaha (North Sumatra) Divination book.

saik galamai (West Sumatra) Ceremonial cake.

sanggori (Sulawesi) Spiral-shaped head ornament.

si gale-gale (North Sumatra) Wooden puppet used in funerals of important persons who died without an heir.

singa (North Sumatra) Composite mythical creature that combines aspects of the water buffalo, the horse, and the *naga* serpent-dragon.

siraha salawa (Nias) Carved figure that represents an early or a founding ancestor.

solobean (North Sumatra) Malevolent form of a *begu*.

sombaon (North Sumatra) Spirit of a deceased person (*begu*) in its highest form.

tau-tau (Sulawesi) Figure carved in the likeness of a high-ranking person who has died.

tondi (North Sumatra) Spirit of a person who is still alive.

tunggal panaluan (North Sumatra) Ritual staff that depicts several figures.

tungkot malehat (North Sumatra) Ritual staff surmounted by a single human figure.

tuntun (Borneo) Figurated measuring rod.

References Cited

Adams, Marie Jeanne

1969   *System and Meaning in East Sumba Textile Design: A Study in Traditional Indonesian Art.* New Haven.

Adhyatman, Sumarah

1987   *Kendi.* Jakarta.

Adriani, N., and A. C. Kruyt

1912–14   *De Bare'e-sprekende Toradja's van Midden Celebes.* 3 vols. Batavia.

Amsterdam. Tropenmuseum (Royal Tropical Institute)

1987   *Budaya Indonesia/Kunst en cultuur in Indonesië/Arts and Crafts in Indonesia.* Text by J. H. van Brakel et al. Exhibition catalogue. Amsterdam.

Aragon, Lorraine V.

1991   "Sulawesi." In Taylor and Aragon 1991.

Ave, Jan B.

1988   "Baby Carrier." In Greub 1988.

Baaren, Th. P. van

1968   *Korwars and Korwar Style.* The Hague.

Barbier, Jean Paul

1983   *Tobaland: The Shreds of Tradition.* Geneva.

1984   *Art of Nagaland.* Exhibition catalogue. Los Angeles: Los Angeles County Museum of Art.

Bartlett, Harley Harris

1934   *The Sacred Edifices of the Batak of Sumatra.* Ann Arbor.

Basel. Museum für Völkerkunde

1930   *Die Inseln Nias und Mentawei* [by Paul Wirz]. Basel.

Baudesson, Henry

[1919?]   *Indo-china and Its Primitive People.* London.

Becker, E.

n.d.   *Die Rheinische Mission in Sumatra.* Barmen [ca. 1922].

Bellwood, Peter

1979   *Man's Conquest of the Pacific: The Prehistory of Southeast Asia and Oceania.* New York.

1985   *Prehistory of the Indo-Malaysian Archipelago.* Sydney.

Brenner, Joachim Freiher von

1894   *Besuch bei den Kannibalen Sumatras.* Würzburg.

Bronson, Bennet

1979   "The Archaeology of Sumatra and the Problem of Srivijaya." In R. B. Smith and W. Watson, eds., *Early South East Asia.* New York.

Brown, Roxanna

1988   *The Ceramics of South-East Asia: Their Dating and Identification.* New York.

Burling, Robbins

1965   *Hill Farms and Padi Fields: Life in Mainland Southeast Asia.* Englewood Cliffs, N.J.

Cameron, Elisabeth L.

1985a   "Ancestor Motifs of the Paiwan." In Feldman 1985.

1985b   "Ancestors and Living Men Among the Batak." In Feldman 1985.

Capistrano-Baker, Florina H.

n.d.   "Under the Sign of the Conquering Calf: Myth and Reality in West Sumatran Architecture." Ph.D. dissertation, Columbia University, New York. Forthcoming.

Ch'en Ch'i-lu

1972   "The Aboriginal Art of Taiwan and Its Implication for the Cultural History of the Pacific." In Noel Barnard and Douglas Fraser, eds., *Early Chinese Art and Its Possible Influence in the Pacific Basin.* New York.

1988   "A Wooden House-Post of the Budai Paiwan." In New York, The Metropolitan Museum of Art, 1988b.

Chin, Lucas

1988   "Trade Objects: Their Impact on the Cultures of the Indigenous Peoples of Sarawak, Borneo." *Expedition* 30, no. 1, pp. 59–64.

Coedès, G.

1962   *Les peuples de la péninsule indochinoise: Histoire — civilisations.* Paris.

1968   *The Indianized States of Southeast Asia.* Edited by W. F. Vella; translated by S. B. Cowing. Honolulu.

Conklin, Harold

1980   *Ethnographic Atlas of Ifugao.* New Haven.

Crystal, Eric

1985   "The Soul That Is Seen: The *Tau Tau* as Shadow of Death, Reflection of Life in Toraja Tradition." In Feldman 1985.

Dallas. Dallas Museum of Art

1982   *Art of the Archaic Indonesians.* Exhibition catalogue. Geneva.

Delft. Volkenkundig Museum Nusantara (formerly the Etnografisch Museum)

1967   *De Bataks op weg.* Introduction by W. Stöhr. Exhibition catalogue. Delft.

1973   *Kalimantan: Mythe en kunst.* Exhibition catalogue. Delft.

1984   *Sieraden en Lichaamsversiering uit Indonesie*, by R. Wassing-Visser. Delft.

1990   *Nias Tribal Treasures: Cosmic Reflections in Stone, Wood, and Gold.* Exhibition catalogue. Delft.

Domeny de Rienzi, Grégoire Louis

1836   *Océanie ou cinquième partie du monde: Revue géographique et ethnographique de la Malaisie, de la Micronésie, de la Polynésie, et de la Mélanesie; offrant les résultats des voyages et des découvertes de l'auteur et de ses devanciers, ainsi que ses nouvelles classifications et divisions de ces contrées.* Paris.

Dournes, Jacques

1968   "La figuration humaine dans l'art funéraire jörai." *Objets et mondes* 8, no. 2, pp. 87–118.

1988   "Autochthonous Peoples of Central Vietnam." In New York, The Metropolitan Museum of Art, 1988b.

Edwards McKinnon, E. P.

1975–77 "Oriental Ceramics Excavated in North Sumatra." *Transactions of the Oriental Ceramic Society* 41, pp. 59–118.

Eliade, Mircea

1964   *Shamanism: Archaic Types of Ecstasy.* Translated by W. R. Trask. New York.

Ellis, George R.

1981   "Art and Peoples of Northern Luzon." In *Arts and Peoples of the Philippines.* Exhibition catalogue. Los Angeles: Museum of Cultural History, UCLA.

Errington, Frederick K.

1984   *Manners and Meaning in West Sumatra: The Social Context of Consciousness.* New Haven.

Feldman, Jerome

1985   Ed. *The Eloquent Dead: Ancestral Sculpture of Indonesia and Southeast Asia.* Exhibition catalogue. Los Angeles: Museum of Cultural History, Frederick S. Wight Art Gallery.

1990   "Nias and Its Traditional Sculptures." In Delft, Volkenkundig Museum Nusantara, 1990.

Fraser-Lu, Sylvia

1989   *Handwoven Textiles of Southeast Asia.* Singapore.

Fürer-Haimendorf, Christoph von

1933   *The Naked Nagas.* Calcutta.

Geertz, Clifford

1963   *Agricultural Involution: The Processes of Ecological Change in Indonesia.* Berkeley and Los Angeles.

Geirnaert, Danielle

1989   "Textiles of West Sumba: The Lively Renaissance of an Old Tradition." In Mattiebelle Gittinger, *To Speak with Cloth: Studies in Indonesian Textiles.* Los Angeles.

Giglioli, Henry Hillyer

1893   "Notes on the Ethnographical Collections, Formed by Dr. Elio Modigliani During His Recent Explorations in Central-Sumatra and Enggano." *Internationales Archiv für Ethnologie* 6, pp. 109–31.

Gittinger, Mattiebelle

1972   "A Study of the Ship Cloths of South Sumatra: Their Design and Usage." Ph.D. dissertation, Columbia University, New York.

Greub, Suzanne, ed.

1988   *Expressions of Belief: Masterpieces of African, Oceanic and Indonesian Art from the Museum voor Volkenkunde, Rotterdam.* Exhibition catalogue. New York.

Grimes, Barbara F.

1988   *Ethnologue: Languages of the World.* Dallas.

Guy, John S.

1986   *Oriental Trade Ceramics in South-East Asia: Ninth to Sixteenth Centuries, with a Catalogue of Chinese, Vietnamese, and Thai Wares in Australian Collections.* Singapore.

Harrisson, Barbara

1979   *Swatow in het Princessehof.* Leeuwarden.

Hauser, Arnold

1985   *The Philosophy of Art History.* Evanston, Ill.

Hein, Alois Raimund

1890   *Die Bildenden Künste bei den Dayaks auf Borneo.* Vienna.

Held, G. J.

1957   *The Papuas of Waropen.* The Hague.

Heppell, Michael, and Limbang Anak Melaka

1988   "Iban Tuntun." *Arts of Asia* 18, no. 2, pp. 64–69.

Heppell, Michael, and Robyn Maxwell

1990   *Borneo and Beyond: Tribal Arts of Indonesia, East Malaysia, and Madagascar.* Singapore: Bareo Gallery.

Hersey, Irwin

1980   "Indonesian Primitive Art." *Arts of Asia* 10, no. 5, pp. 71–87.

1991   *Indonesian Primitive Art.* Singapore and New York.

Hicks, David

1988   "Art and Religion on Timor." In New York, The Metropolitan Museum of Art, 1988b.

Hissink, I.

1912   "Nota van toelichting betreffende de zelfsbesturende landschappen Paloe, Dolo, Sigi, en Biromaroe." *Tijdschrift voor Indische taal-, land-, en volkenkunde* (Batavia) 54.

Hitchcock, Michael

1991   *Indonesian Textiles.* New York.

Ho Ting-jui

1967   "A Comparative Study of Myths and Legends of Formosan Aborigines." 2 vols. Ph.D. dissertation, Indiana University, Bloomington.

Holt, Claire

1967   *Art in Indonesia: Continuities and Change.* Ithaca.

Hoog, J. de

1959   "Nieuwe methoden en inzichten ter bestudering van de funktionele betekenis der beelden in het Indonesisch-Melanesisch kultuurgebied." *Kultuurpatronen* 1, pp. 1–98.

Horsky, R.

1942   "Religiöse Holzplastik auf Nias." *Annalen des Naturhistorischen Museums in Wien*, part 1, vol. 53, pp. 374–98.

Hose, Charles, and William McDougall

1912   *The Pagan Tribes of Borneo.* 2 vols. London.

Jacobs, Julian, et al.

1990   *The Nagas: Hill People of Northeast India.* London.

Jakarta. Direktorat Jenderal Kebudayaan (Departemen Pendidikan dan Kebudayaan)

1980–81   *Seni patung Batak dan Nias*, by M. Saleh. Jakarta.

1984–85   *Patung Pangulubalang di daerah Batak Sumatera Utara.* Jakarta.

Junghuhn, Franz

1847   *Die Battaländer auf Sumatra.* Berlin.

Kartiwa, Suwati

1984   "Adat and Weaving in West Sumatra." M.S. thesis, Graduate School of the University of Pennsylvania, Philadelphia.

1986   *Kain Songket Weaving in Indonesia.* Jakarta.

Kaudern, Walter

1944   *Art in Central Celebes.* Results of the Author's Expedition to Celebes, 1917–20, vol. 6. Göteborg.

Kirch, Patrick J., and Terry L. Hunt, eds.

1988   *Archeology of the Lapita Cultural Complex: A Critical Review.* Seattle.

Leiden, Rijksmuseum voor Volkenkunde

1914   *Katalog des Ethnographischen Reichsmuseums.* Vol. 8, *Bataklander, mit Anhang: Malaiische Länder an der Nordost-Küste Sumatra's [Sumatra II]*, by H. W. Fischer. Leiden.

Loeb, E.

1935   *Sumatra: Its History and People.* Vienna.

Maass, Alfred

1910   *Durch Zentral-Sumatra.* 2 vols. Berlin.

McGovern, Janet B. Montgomery

1923   *Among the Headhunters of Formosa.* Boston.

Madrid

1887   *Exposición General de las Islas Filipinas.* Exhibition catalogue. Madrid.

Man, Edward Horace

n.d.   *The Nicobar Islands and Their People.* London.

1882   "On the Andamanese and Nicobarese Objects Presented to Maj.-Gen. Pitt Rivers, F.R.S." *Journal of the Anthropological Institute of Great Britain and Ireland* 11, pp. 268–90.

1889   "The Nicobar Islanders." *Journal of the Anthropological Institute of Great Britain and Ireland* 18, pp. 354–93.

Marche, Alfred

1886   "Lucon et Palaouan (six années aux Philippines)." *Le tour du monde* (Paris) 1, pp. 177–224.

Marpaung, M., and S. Rodgers

1988a   "Receptacle *(guri-guri).*" In Greub 1988.

1988b   "Female Sculpture." In Greub 1988.

Marschall, W.

1982   "Enggano and Nias." In Dallas, Dallas Museum of Art, 1982.

Maxwell, Robyn J.

1990   *Textiles of Southeast Asia: Tradition, Trade, and Transformation.* [Canberra], Melbourne, and New York.

Meilink-Roelofsz, M. A. P.

1962   *Asian Trade and European Influence in the Indonesian Archipelago Between 1500 and About 1630.* The Hague.

Müller, F. W. K.

1893   "Beschreibung einer von G. Meissner zusammengesammelten Batak-Sammlung." *Veröffentlichungen aus dem Königlichen Museum für Völkerkunde* (Berlin) 3, nos. 1–2.

New York. The Metropolitan Museum of Art

1988a   *Recent Acquisitions: A Selection (1987–1988).* New York.

1988b   *Islands and Ancestors: Indigenous Styles of Southeast Asia.* Edited by Jean Paul Barbier and Douglas Newton. Exhibiton catalogue. New York.

1989   "The Fred and Rita Richman Collection of Southeast Asian Tribal Art." Exhibition, June 13–September 10. No catalogue published.

Ng, Cecilia S. H.

1987   "The Weaving of Prestige: Village Women's Representations of the Social Categories of Minangkabau Society." Ph.D. dissertation, Australian National University, Canberra.

Nieuwenhuis, A. W.

1904   *Quer durch Borneo: Ergebnisse seiner Reisen in den Jahren 1894, 1896–97, und 1898–1900.* Part 1. Leiden.

1907   *Quer durch Borneo: Ergebnisse seiner Reisen in den Jahren 1894, 1896–97, und 1898–1900.* Part 2. Leiden.

Ophuijsen, Ch. A. van

1911   "Der Bataksche Zauberstab." *Internationales Archiv für Ethnographie* 20, no. 3, pp. 82–103.

Palm, C. H. M.

1965   "De Cultuur en Kunst van de Lampung, Sumatra." *Kultuurpatronen* 7, pp. 40–80.

Peralta, Jesus

1977   "Wooden Gods and Other Carvings." In A. R. Roces, ed., *Filipino Heritage: The Making of a Nation,* vol. 2. Manila.

Pichler, Erich

n.d.   "Der Zauberstab und sein Geheimnis: Ein ostasiatisch-ethnographisches Bilderbuch." Manuscript RMG 1346 A/W8H, Archiv der Vereinigten Evangelischen Mission, Wuppertal-Barmen.

Pleyte, C. M.

1894   "L'origine mystique du baton magique en usage chez les Bataks." *T'uong Pao* 1, no. 5, pp. 123–34.

Powell, A. W. B.

1958   "The Canoes of Geelvink Bay, Dutch New Guinea." *Auckland Institute and Museum Records* 5, nos. 1–2, pp. 111–15.

Ramli Dt. Rangkayo Sati

1978   "Pucuak rabuang: Ragam ukiran Minangkabau." Unpublished manuscript, Pandai Sikek, West Sumatra.

Reschke, Heinz

1935 "Die Zauberstabmythen der Batak sind Paradies- und Südenfallerzählungen." *Zeitschrift für Ethnologie* 4, pp. 176–87.

Revel-Macdonald, Nicole

1978 "La danse des hudoq (Kalimantan Timur)." *Objets et mondes* 18, pp. 31–44.

1988 "The Dayak of Borneo: On the Ancestors, the Dead, and the Living." In New York, The Metropolitan Museum of Art, 1988b.

Richman, Rita

1980 "Decorative Household Objects in Indonesia." *Arts of Asia* 10, no. 5, pp. 129–35.

Riedel, J. G. F.

1886 *De sluik- en kroesharige rassen tusschen Celebes en Papua*. The Hague.

Rodgers, Susan

1985 *Power and Gold: Jewelry from Indonesia, Malaysia, and the Philippines from the Collection of the Barbier-Müller Museum, Geneva*. Exhibition catalogue. Geneva: Barbier-Müller Museum; New York: Asia Society.

1988 "Priest's Wand *(tunggal panaluan)*." In Greub 1988.

Roth, H. Ling

1896 *The Natives of Sarawak and British North Borneo*. London.

Rowney, Horatio Bickerstaffe

1882 *The Wild Tribes of India*. London.

Sarasin, Paul, and Fritz Sarasin

1905 *Reisen in Celebes*. 2 vols. Wiesbaden.

Schnitger, F. M.

1939 *Forgotten Kingdoms in Sumatra*. Leiden.

Schoffel, Alain

1981 *Arts primitifs de l'Asie du Sud-Est (Assam, Sumatra, Bornéo, Philippines): Collection Alain Schoffel*. Meudon. Text in French and English.

Schröder, E. E. W. Gs.

1917 *Nias: Ethnographische, geographische, en historische aanteekeningen en studiën*. 2 vols. Leiden.

Sellato, Bernard

1989 *Hornbill and Dragon*. Malaysia.

Sibeth, Achim

1991 *The Batak: Peoples of the Island of Sumatra*. London and New York. First published in German in 1990.

Singapore. Southeast Asian Ceramic Society

1979 *Chinese Celadons and Other Related Wares in Southeast Asia*. Singapore.

Soedjatmoko, Mohammad Ali, G. J. Resink, and G. McT. Kahin, eds.

1965 *An Introduction to Indonesian Historiography*. Ithaca.

Solheim, Wilhelm G., II

1981 "Philippine Prehistory." In *Arts and Peoples of the Philippines*. Exhibition catalogue. Los Angeles: Museum of Cultural History, UCLA.

1985 "*Korwar* of the Biak." In Feldman 1985.

Steinmann, A.

1965a "Das Schiff in der darstellenden Kunst Südostasiens." *Kultuurpatronen* 7, pp. 12–22.

1965b "Das Seelenschiff in der Textilkunst Indonesiens." *Kultuurpatronen* 7, pp. 23–39.

Summerfield, Anne, and John Summerfield

1991 *Fabled Cloths of Minangkabau*. Exhibition catalogue. Santa Barbara: Santa Barbara Museum of Art.

Svoboda, W.

1893 "Die Bewohner des Nikobaren-Archipels." *Internationales Archiv für Ethnographie* 6, pp. 1–40.

Taylor, Paul Michael

1988 "From *Mantra* to *Mataráa*: Opacity and Transparency in the Language of Tobelo Magic and Medicine (Halmahera Island, Indonesia)." In Beatrix Pfleiderer, ed., "Permanence and Change in Asian Health Care Traditions," *Social Science and Medicine* 27, no. 5, pp. 425–36.

1994a Ed. *Fragile Traditions: Indonesian Art in Jeopardy*. Honolulu.

1994b "Indonesia: Jewel in the Crown." In Frank H. Talbot, *Islands*. Sydney.

Taylor, Paul Michael, and Lorraine V. Aragon

1991 *Beyond the Java Sea: Art of Indonesia's Outer Islands*. Exhibition catalogue. Washington, D.C.: National Museum of Natural History, Smithsonian Institution.

Villaverde, Juan

1909 "The Ifugaos of Quiangan and Vicinity," translated and edited by Dean C. Worcester. *Philippine Journal of Science* 4, no. 4 (1909), pp. 237–65. First published in Spanish in 1879.

Voorhoeve, P.

n.d.   "Two Batak Tree-Bark Manuscripts." *Musée Barbier-Müller, Geneva, Connaissance des arts tribaux, bulletin,* no. 13 [198-].

Vroklage, B. A. G.

1952   *Ethnographie der Belu in Zentral-Timor.* 3 vols. Leiden.

Warneck, Johannes

1909   *Die Religion der Batak: Ein Paradigma für die animistischen Religionen des Indischen Archipels.* Göttingen.

Whittier, Herbert L., and Patricia R. Whittier

1988   "Baby Carriers: A Link Between Social and Spiritual Values." *Expedition* 30, no. 1, pp. 51–58.

Winkler, Johannes

1925   *Die Toba-Batak auf Sumatra in gesunden und kranken Tagen.* Stuttgart.

Wirz, Otto

1929   *Nias: Die Insel der Götzen.* Zurich and Leipzig.

Wuppertal-Barmen. Vereinigte Evangelische Mission

n.d   *Die Rheinische Mission auf Nias.* Wuppertal-Barmen.

Wurm, S. A., and S. Hattori

1983   *Language Atlas of the Pacific Area.* Part 2. Canberra.

Ydema, J. M.

1966   "Aantekeningen bij het Toba-Batakse huismasker en andere Batakse voorwerpen, hoofdzakelijk in verband met de Hagedis. . . ." *Kultuurpatronen* 8, pp. 5–78.